Canon EOS R7 User Guide

Master Camera Settings, Autofocus, and 4K Video with Step-by-Step Lessons, Real-Life Shooting Tips, and Quick Cheat Sheets for Beginners, Seniors & Enthusiasts

Randy Osborn

Disclaimer:

This book is an independent publication and is not affiliated with, authorized, sponsored, or endorsed by Canon Inc. or any of its subsidiaries.

All product names, logos, brands, and trademarks mentioned in this guide are the property of their respective owners. References to "Canon," "Canon EOS R7," and any related terms are used strictly for identification and descriptive purposes only, to refer to the camera model that this guide is designed to help users understand and operate.

While every effort has been made to ensure the accuracy and clarity of the information presented, the author and publisher assume no responsibility for errors, omissions, or any outcomes resulting from the application of the techniques or tips described in this book. Camera models, features, software, and firmware updates may change over time. Always consult the official Canon documentation or website for the most current product specifications and instructions.

This guide is intended for educational and informational purposes only.

How to Use This Book

The Canon EOS R7 is an extraordinary camera. It has the speed of a sports body, the precision of Canon's Dual Pixel autofocus, and the flexibility to capture everything from wildlife to cinematic 4K video. But here's the truth most manuals won't tell you: if you try to learn it all at once, you'll feel overwhelmed. Menus seem endless. Acronyms blur together. And instead of creating the images you imagined, you risk leaving the camera on Auto and never unlocking its full potential.

That's exactly why this guide exists — to walk you through the EOS R7 in a way that feels practical, achievable, and even enjoyable. Think of it less as a manual and more as a personal coach who will stand beside you as you learn, answering your questions, pointing out shortcuts, and giving you confidence at every step.

Here's how this book is designed for you:

1. Step-by-Step Learning

You'll never be thrown into technical jargon without a clear path forward. Each chapter is broken into bite-sized lessons, guiding you from the absolute basics — inserting your first battery, attaching a lens, finding your way around the menus — to more advanced skills like customizing buttons, mastering autofocus tracking, or shooting 4K video. Every step builds on the one before it, so you're always moving forward with clarity.

2. Shooting "Recipes" for Real-Life Situations

Photography isn't about memorizing menus; it's about capturing moments. That's why throughout the book you'll find practical shooting recipes — simple, repeatable setups for real-world scenarios.

- Want a crisp portrait of your child? There's a recipe for that.

- Need to track a bird in flight? You'll learn the exact autofocus mode and shutter speed.

- Planning to vlog or shoot a travel reel? Follow the video recipe and you'll be ready in minutes.

These recipes cut through the overwhelm and tell you exactly what settings to use and why, so you can focus on creating instead of guessing.

3. Quick Fixes & Troubleshooting

Every photographer — beginner or expert — runs into frustrating moments. Photos come out blurry. The camera refuses to focus. A memory card throws an error just when you need it most. Instead of flipping through dense manuals, this guide gives you quick fixes right where you need them. Clear, simple instructions will help you solve the problem in seconds and get back to shooting with confidence.

4. Cheat Sheets for Fast Reference

Sometimes you don't want explanations; you just need answers. That's why I've included one-page cheat sheets at the end of the book. These are shortcuts for when you're in the field or traveling:

- Autofocus modes explained at a glance.

- ISO and exposure quick reference.

- Video setup shortcuts.

- Lens recommendations for every situation.

Keep them bookmarked or even photocopy them — they're designed to save you time when the moment matters.

5. Learn at Your Own Pace

This book isn't meant to be read in one sitting. Instead, treat it like a toolbox: pick it up when you're learning something new, stuck on a problem, or preparing for a specific type of shoot. Beginners may choose to read straight through, building their skills chapter by chapter. More experienced photographers may dip into the shooting recipes or cheat sheets as needed. However you use it, the goal is the same — to help you make the most of your Canon EOS R7 and unlock the images and videos you've been imagining.

6. Build Confidence, Not Just Knowledge

By the time you finish this guide, you won't just know what every button or menu option does — you'll feel confident putting them into practice. You'll understand when to switch AF modes, how to adapt settings in tricky lighting, and how to prepare for your next big shoot. More importantly, you'll no longer feel like the camera is smarter than you. You'll be the one in control.

In short, use this book as your step-by-step roadmap, your recipe collection, your problem solver, and your quick-reference companion.

Whenever you feel lost, it will bring you back on track. Whenever you want to try something new, it will give you the courage to experiment. And whenever you need inspiration, it will remind you why you picked up the EOS R7 in the first place: to create images and stories that matter.

Table of Contents

Preface

The Canon EOS R7 is one of the most versatile mirrorless cameras Canon has ever created, and this Canon EOS R7 User Guide is the companion every photographer needs to unlock its full potential. Whether you're completely new to digital photography or upgrading to a more advanced system, this is more than just an EOS R7 manual — it's a step-by-step Canon R7 camera guide written in plain English, designed to make complex features simple.

Inside this Canon EOS R7 photography book, you'll find everything you need to move from first setup to confident shooting. Think of it as a hands-on Canon EOS R7 tutorial that walks you through the EOS R7 setup and settings, explains the menus clearly, and gives you real-life tips on how to use Canon EOS R7 for any subject.

You'll master the R7's autofocus system with a dedicated Canon EOS R7 autofocus guide, learning how to use Face and Eye Detection, how to choose between One Shot vs Servo AF, and why

Canon EOS R7 autofocus explained in practical terms matters for portraits, sports, and wildlife. You'll discover recommended Canon EOS R7 wildlife photography settings, flattering portrait photography settings, and fast-paced sports and action settings. For filmmakers and content creators, there's a full breakdown of Canon EOS R7 video settings, including slow motion video setup, C-Log profiles, and even tips for the EOS R7 autofocus and video settings that professionals rely on.

This isn't just theory — it's a Canon EOS R7 quick start guide packed with Canon EOS R7 tips and tricks that show you exactly how to get better results in the real world. From Canon EOS R7 menu explained in simple language, to understanding the EOS R7 exposure triangle, you'll learn to balance aperture, shutter speed, and ISO with confidence. You'll also find solutions to common frustrations, such as the Canon EOS R7 overheating fix, how to choose the right Canon EOS R7 lenses recommended, and the best accessories for Canon EOS R7 that make a big difference in everyday shooting.

For learners looking for a solid foundation, this book doubles as a digital photography for beginners resource and a mirrorless camera photography guide, offering the same clarity you'd expect from a trusted Canon photography guidebook, a beginner's photography manual, or a true digital camera guide. Each chapter is written for real photographers — with examples, practice "recipes," and photography tips for beginners that help you understand not just the settings, but how to shoot better photos in practice.

No matter your passion — portraits, landscapes, wildlife, or content creation — you'll find clear step-by-step help here. Learn landscape photography settings for sunrise and sunset, follow a wildlife photography camera guide for capturing birds in flight, or explore vlogging and content creation with Canon cameras for YouTube and social media success.

Because the R7 is sold worldwide, this guide is also a practical Canon EOS R7 handbook, a reliable Canon EOS R7 instruction manual, and a go-to Canon EOS R7 guidebook. International readers will find it just as valuable under the names Canon EOS R7 Handbuch, Canon EOS R7 manual de usuario, or Canon EOS R7 guida fotografica. No matter how you search for help, this book ensures you'll find answers.

Written in a friendly, jargon-free style, this guide is perfect for mirrorless photography beginners who want clear instruction, and equally useful for enthusiasts ready to push their skills further. With its blend of Canon tutorial style walkthroughs, practical cheat sheets, and creative exercises, this book gives you everything you need to move beyond auto mode and start shooting with confidence.

If you've been looking for the one resource that makes the Canon EOS R7 simple, approachable, and powerful — this is it.

Introduction

When you first hold the Canon EOS R7 in your hands, you feel the promise of possibility. It's more than just a camera — it's a gateway into storytelling, memory-making, and seeing the world in a new way. But like any powerful tool, the R7 can feel overwhelming at first. So many buttons, menus, and modes. So much potential. Where do you even begin?

That's where this guide comes in.

This book was written to do more than explain technical details. It's designed to be your mentor on the page — breaking down every feature of the EOS R7 into clear, practical steps you can follow. No jargon for jargon's sake. No unnecessary complexity. Just plain-English explanations, real-world scenarios, and hands-on "recipes" that help you go from fumbling with settings to capturing the photos and videos you imagined.

Inside, you'll discover:

- How to set up your R7 for the very first time and take your first photo in minutes.

- What every button, dial, and touchscreen shortcut does — explained simply.

- How to master exposure, autofocus, and color so your images consistently look sharp and vibrant.

- Practical shooting recipes for family portraits, wildlife, travel, sports, landscapes, vlogs, and even the night sky.

- Video tools like oversampled 4K, slow motion, and Canon Log 3, explained for beginners and creators alike.

- Hidden features, efficiency tips, and quick fixes that even seasoned photographers sometimes overlook.

And because photography isn't just about theory, this book is filled with pictorial guides and cheat sheets — visual quick references you can glance at in the field to remind you what settings to use when.

Whether you're new to interchangeable-lens cameras, moving up from an older Canon body, or simply eager to unlock the EOS R7's full potential, this guide meets you where you are and walks you forward. You don't need to be a "tech person." You don't need years of experience. You just need curiosity, a willingness to practice, and the right guidance.

The Canon EOS R7 is a camera that rewards practice with results. It was built for flexibility — fast enough for wildlife and sports, refined enough for portraits and landscapes, compact enough for travel, and powerful enough for professional video. But it doesn't shine on its own. It shines in your hands, when you learn how to make it respond to your vision.

This book is your shortcut to that moment — the moment when you stop thinking about buttons and start seeing photographs before you even lift the camera to your eye.

So, take a deep breath. Open to the first chapter. And let's begin the journey of turning the EOS R7 from a complex machine into your creative partner.

Chapter 1

Getting Started with Your EOS R7

Unboxing a new camera is an exciting moment. The Canon EOS R7 is more than just a piece of technology — it's a creative partner, capable of freezing moments in razor-sharp detail, tracking wildlife with astonishing precision, and delivering professional-grade 4K video. But as with any advanced camera, the first steps matter. Setting it up correctly from the start will save you hours of frustration and ensure you're ready to capture images that match the vision in your mind.

In this chapter, we'll walk through everything you need to get started: unboxing, preparing your camera for its first use, understanding the basic menu system, configuring the most important settings, and even taking your very first photograph.

Unboxing and First Setup

When you open the Canon EOS R7 box, you'll typically find:

- The camera body (with a protective body cap attached).

- A Canon LP-E6NH rechargeable battery pack.

- A battery charger.

- A Canon strap.

- A USB cable.

- The user manual and warranty information.

Depending on where you purchased it, your box may also include a kit lens such as the RF-S 18-150mm or RF-S 18-45mm. If not, you'll need to have a compatible Canon RF or RF-S lens ready.

1. Insert the Battery

Flip the camera over and slide the battery compartment latch open. Insert the LP-E6NH battery, ensuring the terminals align properly, then close the cover until it clicks. A brand-new battery may not be fully charged; it's best to charge it completely before your first outing.

2. Insert a Memory Card

The EOS R7 uses SD UHS-II cards for optimal speed. Slide open the memory card door on the side of the camera. Insert the card with the label facing the back of the camera until it clicks into place. Close the door firmly.

3. Mount a Lens

Remove the body cap from the camera and the rear cap from your lens. Align the red dot on the lens mount with the red dot on the camera body (or the white square if you're attaching an RF-S lens). Gently twist clockwise until the lens locks into place with a click. Always avoid dust or fingerprints entering the sensor area.

4. Power On the Camera

Turn the power switch, located near the top right, from OFF to ON. The LCD screen will light up, and you'll be greeted with the first setup screen.

5. Check for Firmware Updates

Canon periodically releases firmware updates to improve autofocus, fix bugs, or add features. Connect to Canon's website, download the latest firmware onto your memory card, and update via the camera's setup menu. It's optional for day one, but it's worth ensuring your EOS R7 runs the latest version.

Navigating the Menu System in Plain English

The EOS R7's menu is comprehensive — and, at first glance, intimidating. Don't worry. You don't need to memorize every option. What matters is knowing how the menus are structured.

- **Red Tabs (Shooting Menus):** Control image quality, exposure settings, autofocus behavior, and drive modes.

- **Blue Tabs (Playback Menus):** Settings for reviewing and protecting your images.

- **Yellow Tabs (Setup Menus):** Adjust date/time, display brightness, card formatting, firmware updates.

- **Green Tab (My Menu):** Your personal customizable menu — where you'll eventually store your most-used options.

- **Orange Tabs (AF, Playback, Network):** Specialized settings for autofocus, wireless connectivity, and advanced functions.

Navigation is simple: use the joystick, touchscreen, or control dial to move through options. Press SET (the center button on the rear wheel) to confirm a choice. You'll get used to the layout quickly, especially with practice.

First-Time Setup Checklist

When you power on the EOS R7 for the first time, it will prompt you to set up key functions. Here's the checklist to get you going smoothly:

1. **Set Date, Time, and Time Zone**

   Accurate timestamps help organize your photos later, especially if you shoot travel or multiple events in one day.

2. **Choose Image Quality**

- Select *RAW + JPEG* if you want maximum flexibility (ideal for editing).

- Select *JPEG* if you're a beginner and want smaller, ready-to-use files.

- *HEIF* format is also available for higher quality compressed files, though not all computers support it.

3. **Set Card Recording Options**

   The EOS R7 has two card slots. You can choose:

- **Standard recording:** Fill one card, then switch to the other.

- **Simultaneous recording:** Save the same image to both cards (backup).

- **RAW/JPEG split:** RAW files on one card, JPEGs on the other.

For beginners, "Standard" mode is easiest.

4. **Format Your Memory Card**

Always format a new card before use to ensure compatibility. This option is in the yellow *Setup* menu.

5. **Set Default Shooting Mode**

Turn the mode dial to P (Program Auto) for your first shots. This gives the camera control over exposure but lets you adjust other settings.

6. **Enable Touchscreen & Grid Display**

The touchscreen makes navigating menus faster. The grid display helps with composition.

Quick Start: Take Your First Photo in Under 5 Minutes

By now your battery, card, and lens should be in place, and your basic settings configured. Here's how to capture your very first shot:

1. Turn the mode dial to P (Program Auto).

2. Raise the camera to your eye or use the LCD screen.

3. Frame your subject (a person, pet, or object nearby).

4. Half-press the shutter button. The camera will focus automatically. A green box will appear to confirm focus.

5. Fully press the shutter button to take the photo.

6. Review your image by pressing the Play button.

Congratulations — you've just captured your first photograph with the Canon EOS R7.

Building Momentum

This chapter is about making the EOS R7 feel approachable. From here, you'll start to experiment: switching modes, testing autofocus, and customizing controls. But the most important step is already behind you — you've unboxed, set up, configured, and fired your first shot. Each chapter that follows will build on this foundation, taking you deeper into the camera's extraordinary capabilities.

So, keep your camera close at hand. By the time you finish this book, the EOS R7 will no longer feel like a new purchase. It will feel like an extension of your eye, ready to translate your vision into unforgettable images.

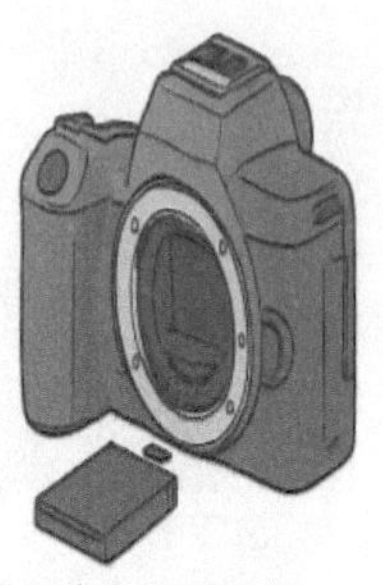

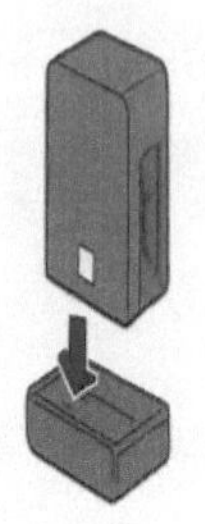

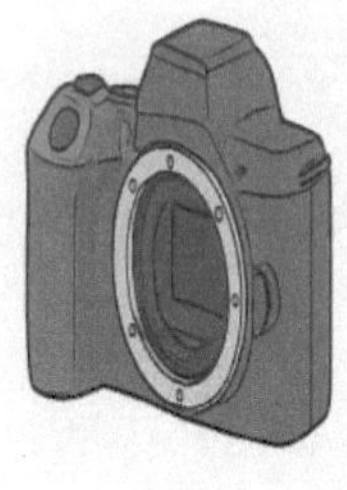

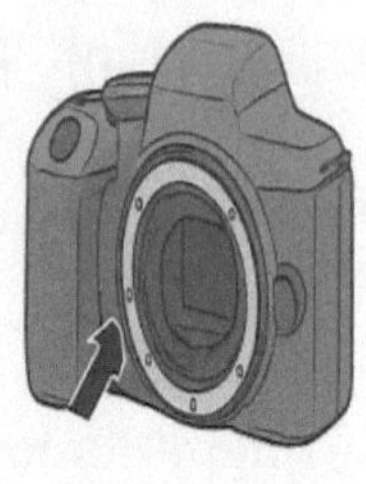

Insert the battery into the compartment at the base of the camera until it clicks securely in place

Slide your SD card into the slot with the label facing the rear screen until it locks in place

Slide your SD card into the slot with the label facinag the rear screen until it locks in place

Switch the power dial to ON to activate your EOS R7

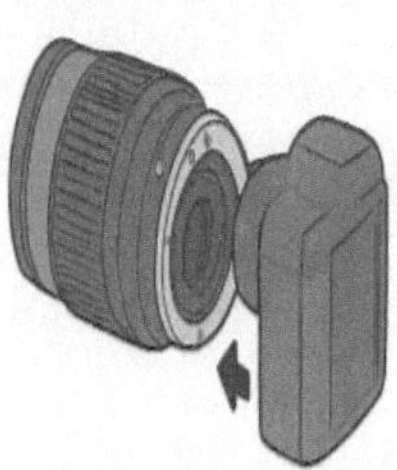

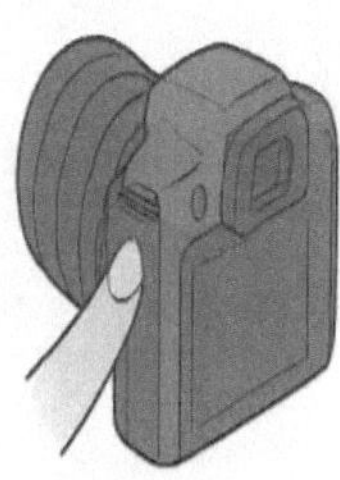

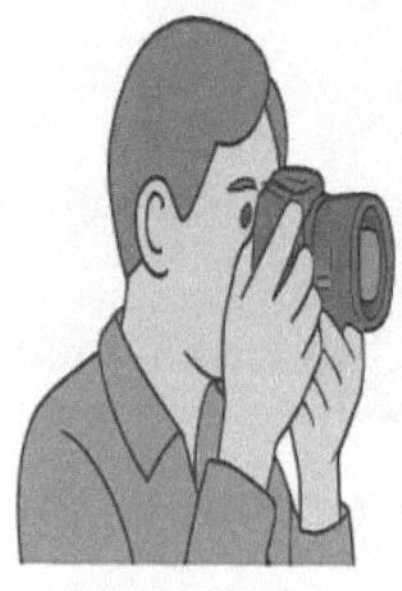

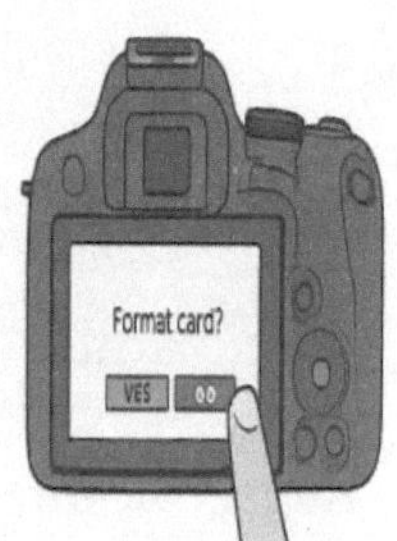

Use the touchscreen or joystick to move through the menu tabs, red for shooting, yellow for setup, blue for playback, green cun-

Always format your card in-camera before use to avoid errors

Half press the shutter to focus, then fully press to capture your first image

Press the Play button to instantly review your image on the screen

Chapter 2

Exploring Buttons, Dials & Touchscreen

Every camera is like a new language. Before you can tell stories through photos and video, you need to learn the alphabet — the buttons, dials, and controls that make up your Canon EOS R7. At first glance, the body might look covered in switches and icons, but don't worry: each one has a clear purpose, and once you've practiced, they'll become second nature.

Think of this chapter as your guided tour of the R7's body. You'll learn what every button and dial does, how the touchscreen adds a modern twist, and even how to personalize controls so the camera feels like it was built for you. By the end, you'll be able to operate the R7 without hesitation, freeing you to focus on creativity rather than fumbling for settings.

Camera Body Tour

Let's start by walking around the EOS R7 and identifying its main areas:

Front of the Camera:

- **Lens Mount & Release Button:** The large circular mount is where you attach RF or RF-S lenses. The small round button on the side releases the lens when you want to change it.

- **AF Assist Lamp / Self-Timer Lamp:** A tiny light that helps autofocus in dim settings and flashes when using the self-timer.

- **Grip:** Shaped for comfort, this is where your right hand naturally rests. Inside, the shutter button awaits your touch.

Top of the Camera:

- **Mode Dial:** This is the command center for choosing how you shoot: Auto, Program, Aperture Priority, Shutter Priority, Manual, and custom modes (C1–C3).

- **Main Control Dial:** Just behind the shutter button, this dial adjusts settings like aperture or shutter speed depending on your mode.

- **Multi-Function (M-Fn) Button:** Located next to the shutter, this button gives quick access to customizable settings such as ISO, white balance, or drive mode.

- **On/Off Switch:** Powers the camera. Simple but essential.

- **Hot Shoe:** A mount for attaching external flashes, microphones, or other accessories.

Back of the Camera:

- **Electronic Viewfinder (EVF):** The eyepiece that shows you exactly what the sensor sees. High resolution and responsive.

- **Rear Control Dial:** Positioned next to the viewfinder, this dial is handy for changing settings with your thumb.

- **Joystick (Multi-Controller):** Lets you move autofocus points around quickly.

- **AF-ON Button:** Commonly used for back-button focusing — a pro trick that separates focusing from shooting.

- **Q/Set Button (inside the rear dial):** Press this to bring up the Quick Menu for on-screen settings.

- **Menu Button:** Access the full camera menu system.

- **Playback Button:** Review your photos and videos.

- **Trash/Delete Button:** Removes unwanted images.

- **Info Button:** Cycles through different display options on the LCD or EVF.

LCD Screen:

- A fully articulating touchscreen that flips out for selfies, vlogging, or tricky angles. It doubles as a live-view display and a menu navigator.

What Each Button and Dial Does, Explained Simply

Cameras can feel intimidating because every control seems to have a symbol. Let's break them down in plain English:

- **Shutter Button (top right):** Half-press to focus, full press to take a photo.

- **Mode Dial (top left):** Decides who's in charge — you or the camera. Use Auto for hands-off shooting, P for balance, Av/Tv for creative control, and M for full manual.

- **Main Dial (next to shutter):** Adjusts aperture or shutter speed depending on mode.

- **Rear Dial (thumb wheel):** Works with the main dial for quick setting changes.

- **Joystick (multi-controller):** Move your focus point exactly where you want it.

- **AF-ON Button:** Lets you focus with your thumb instead of the shutter button — faster and more accurate for many shooters.

- **Q/Set Button:** Shortcut to adjust settings on-screen without diving into full menus.

- **Playback & Trash:** Self-explanatory — view and manage your shots.

- **Info Button:** Customize what info appears in your viewfinder/LCD, like histogram or grid lines.

Every button is there to help you work faster. At first, you'll look down often to find them. But after a week or two of use, muscle memory will kick in, and your fingers will instinctively know where to go.

Touchscreen Tips and Hidden Shortcuts

The EOS R7's touchscreen is one of its biggest advantages. Unlike older DSLR-style bodies, you can tap, swipe, and pinch just like on a smartphone. Here's how to make the most of it:

- **Touch to Focus:** Tap anywhere on the screen to instantly move your focus point. Perfect for portraits, product shots, or off-center subjects.

- **Pinch to Zoom (Playback Mode):** Use two fingers to zoom in and check sharpness.

- **Swipe to Scroll:** Quickly flick through photos in playback.

- **Quick Menu Access:** Press the **Q** button, then use touch to change ISO, white balance, or drive mode without fumbling through menus.

- **Drag AF (when using the EVF):** Set the screen as a touchpad while your eye is on the viewfinder. Drag your thumb to move the AF point without lifting your eye.

- *Hidden Shortcut:* Double-tap the screen during live view to magnify focus on your subject. Handy for macro photography.

Personalizing Controls: Why It Matters for Faster Shooting

One of the EOS R7's greatest strengths is customization. You don't have to use the buttons and dials the way Canon set them up. You can assign them to match your style. Why does this matter? Because photography is about speed and flow. The less you think about menus, the faster you capture the moment.

Here's how personalization can help:

- **Back-Button Focus (BBF):** Assign AF to the AF-ON button, freeing your shutter for taking photos only. This technique improves accuracy in action and wildlife shots.

- **Custom Functions (C1, C2, C3 on the mode dial):** Save complete setups for specific scenarios. Example: C1 for portraits, C2 for landscapes, C3 for video.

- **My Menu (Green Tab):** Create your own menu page with your most-used settings — no more hunting through tabs.

- **Reassigning Buttons:** For example, you can make the M-Fn button change ISO instead of its default.

- *Pro Insight:* Personalization is what makes the camera disappear between you and your subject. Once controls are mapped to your habits, shooting becomes seamless.

Bringing It All Together

You've just completed a guided tour of the EOS R7's controls. At first, this may feel like a lot — front buttons, back dials, touchscreen shortcuts, personalization options. But remember: you don't need to master them all at once. Begin with the essentials (shutter, mode dial, joystick, Q/Set button), then add new shortcuts as you grow comfortable.

In time, you'll no longer think about where your fingers go. Instead, your hands will move instinctively, leaving your eyes free to compose and your mind free to create. That's when the R7 transforms from a tool into an extension of you.

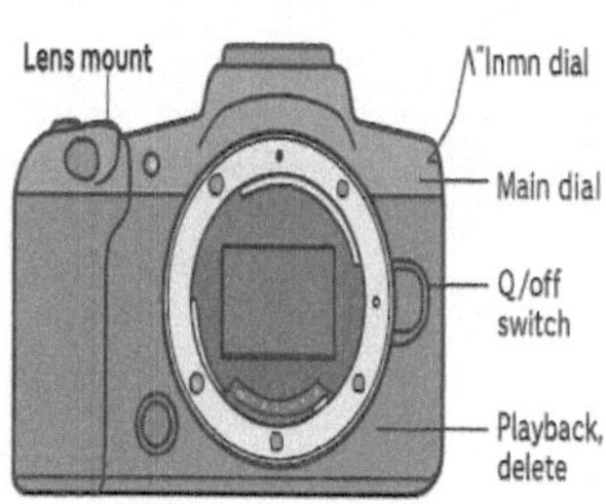

Front view: lens mount, release button, AF assist lamp, and ergonomic grip

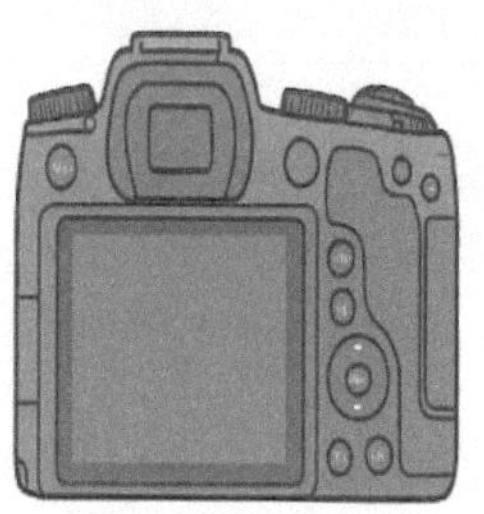

Back view: electronic viewfinder, joystick, A FON, Q/Set button

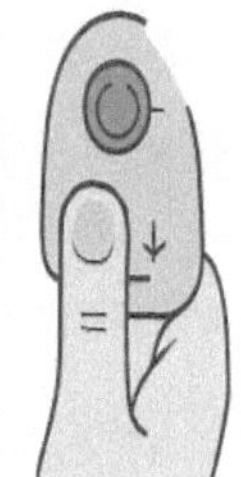

Half-press to focus, full press to capture

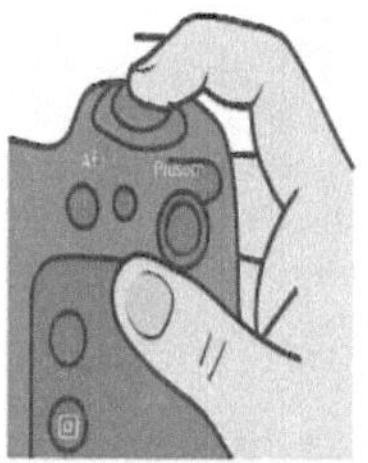

Half-press to focus, full press to capture

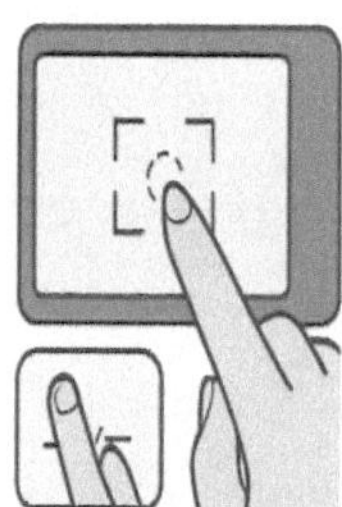

Tap to focus, swipe to navigate, pinch to zoom

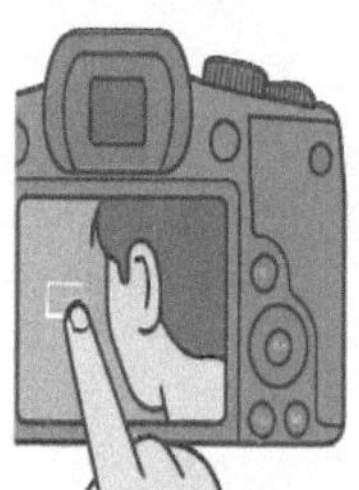

Assign focus to ia the AF-ON button for faster, more accurate shooting

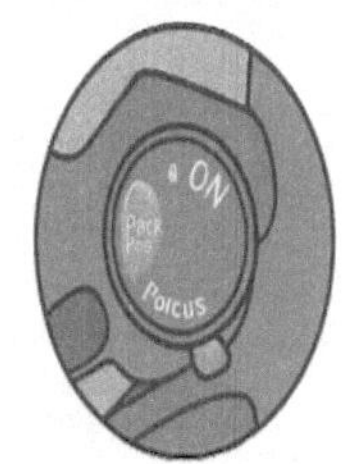

Save your favorite setups to C1, C2, and C3 for instant recall

Chapter 3

The Exposure Triangle Made Simple

If photography is a language, then exposure is its grammar. Exposure determines how bright or dark your image looks, and how well it captures detail in highlights and shadows. Too much exposure, and your image is washed out; too little, and it's buried in darkness.

The Canon EOS R7 has a highly intelligent sensor and processor that can handle exposure beautifully on its own. But to step beyond Auto and truly control your photography, you need to understand the exposure triangle: aperture, shutter speed, and ISO. These three elements work together like the legs of a tripod. Change one, and you affect the balance of the others.

The good news? You don't need to drown in jargon to master it. By the end of this chapter, you'll know how to use these three tools with confidence, when to use exposure compensation, which modes make sense for your situation, and how to practice until it feels natural.

Aperture: Controlling Depth and Light

Aperture is the opening inside your lens. It works like the pupil in your eye — it widens in low light to let more in and narrows in bright light to limit it. On your R7, aperture is expressed as f-numbers (f/2.8, f/4, f/11, etc.).

- **Lower f-number (f/2.8, f/4):** A wide opening. More light enters, and you get a shallow depth of field. This means your subject is sharp but the background blurs beautifully — perfect for portraits or close-ups.

- **Higher f-number (f/11, f/16):** A narrow opening. Less light enters, and you get a deeper depth of field. More of the scene stays in focus — ideal for landscapes.

Quick Tip: Think of aperture as "background control." Wide apertures blur the background; narrow apertures keep more in focus.

Shutter Speed: Freezing or Blurring Motion

Shutter speed is how long the camera's shutter stays open to let light in. It's measured in fractions of a second (1/500, 1/60, 1/4) or whole seconds for long exposures.

- **Fast shutter speeds (1/1000, 1/2000):** Freeze action. Perfect for sports, birds in flight, or kids running.

- **Moderate speeds (1/60, 1/125):** Good for everyday handheld shots.

- **Slow speeds (1/4, 1 second, 30 seconds):** Allow more light in, but risk blur unless you use a tripod. These speeds are used for creative effects like smooth waterfalls, night trails, or low-light cityscapes.

Quick Tip: Ask yourself, "Am I freezing motion or showing motion?" That's your shutter speed decision.

ISO: The Sensor's Sensitivity

ISO controls how sensitive your camera's sensor is to light. Lower ISO = less sensitivity, cleaner images. Higher ISO = more sensitivity, brighter images, but with more digital noise (grain).

- **ISO 100–400:** Best for daylight. Clean and crisp.

- **ISO 800–1600:** Good for indoors or evening.

- **ISO 3200–6400+:** For very low light. Usable, but you'll start to see noise.

Quick Tip: Always start at the lowest ISO you can, and only raise it when light demands it.

Putting It Together: The Triangle

Aperture, shutter speed, and ISO always work together to create the final exposure. If you open the aperture wide (f/2.8), you let in more light — so you can either use a faster shutter or lower ISO. If you raise ISO, you can use a faster shutter but risk noise. Adjusting one means balancing the others.

Think of it as three sliders. If one moves up, another usually has to move down.

Exposure Compensation: Fine-Tuning the Balance

Even in Auto or semi-automatic modes, your R7's meter sometimes misjudges a scene. Bright snow may look gray; a backlit subject may come out too dark. That's where exposure compensation (EC) comes in.

Exposure compensation is like telling the camera, "Make it brighter" (+1 or +2) or "Make it darker" (−1 or −2). On the R7, you adjust EC with a dedicated dial or through the touchscreen.

- **Use + EC:** To brighten underexposed shots (faces in shadow, backlit subjects).

- **Use – EC:** To darken overexposed shots (snow, white sand, bright skies).

Pro Insight: Exposure compensation doesn't change your aperture, shutter, or ISO settings directly; it nudges the camera to bias the exposure brighter or darker while staying in Auto or semi-auto modes.

Auto vs Semi-Auto vs Manual Modes

The mode dial on your R7 gives you choices for how much control you want:

- **Auto (green mode):** The camera does everything. Good for emergencies, but it limits creativity.

- **Program (P):** Camera sets aperture and shutter, you can shift settings and adjust ISO/EC. A safety net for beginners.

- **Aperture Priority (Av):** You choose the aperture, the camera adjusts shutter speed. Great for controlling background blur.

- **Shutter Priority (Tv):** You choose shutter speed, the camera picks aperture. Great for sports or motion effects.

- **Manual (M):** You control all three: aperture, shutter, ISO. Best for learning and full creative control.

Beginner Strategy: Start in Av for portraits and landscapes, Tv for action, then practice in M when you feel comfortable.

Step-by-Step: Practice Exercises to Nail Exposure

Knowledge only sticks when you use it. Here are simple exercises you can try with your EOS R7:

Exercise 1: Aperture Control

1. Switch to Av mode.

2. Take the same portrait at f/4, f/8, and f/16.

3. Compare how the background changes from blurred to sharp.

Exercise 2: Shutter Control

1. Switch to Tv mode.

2. Photograph moving water or passing cars at 1/1000, 1/60, and 1/4.

3. Notice how fast speeds freeze motion while slow speeds create blur.

Exercise 3: ISO Impact

1. Shoot the same scene indoors at ISO 100, 800, and 3200.

2. Compare noise levels in the darker areas of your photos.

Exercise 4: Exposure Compensation

1. In Av mode, point at a bright wall or snowy scene.

2. Take one photo at 0 EC, one at +1, one at −1.

3. Compare brightness and decide which matches your vision.

Exercise 5: Manual Balance

1. Switch to M mode.

2. Set ISO to 100.

3. Adjust aperture and shutter speed until the exposure meter inside the viewfinder is balanced at zero.

4. Take the shot, then intentionally shift +1 and −1 to see the effect.

Repeat these often, and you'll find exposure decisions become second nature.

Closing Thoughts

Mastering the exposure triangle is like learning to ride a bike. At first, balancing three controls feels awkward. But soon, it clicks — you won't even think about ISO, aperture, or shutter; you'll just *know* what to do.

Your EOS R7 is a powerful partner in this process. It offers guidance through Auto and semi-auto modes, but also the freedom to go fully manual when you're ready. With practice, you'll discover the joy of not just capturing what you see, but shaping it to look exactly how you imagined.

Exposure is your creative paintbrush. Learn to use it, and the world becomes your canvas.

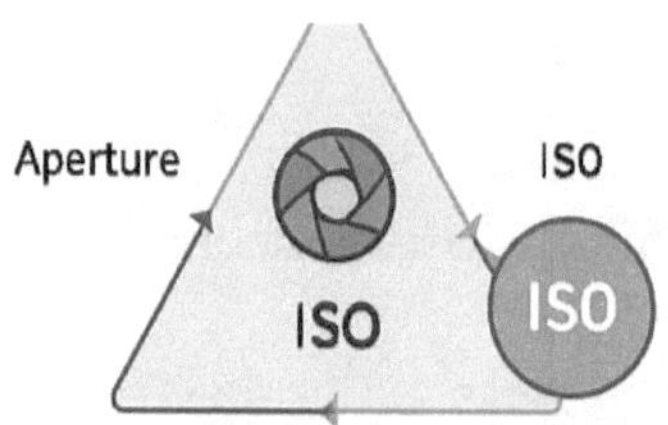

The exposure triangle: apertture, shutter speed, and ISO working together to control brightness.

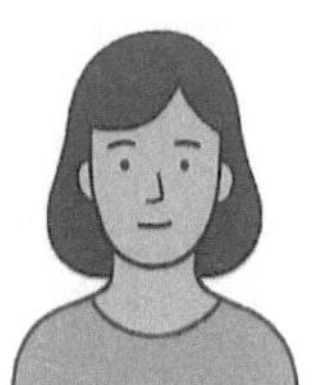

Wide apertures blur the backgront;

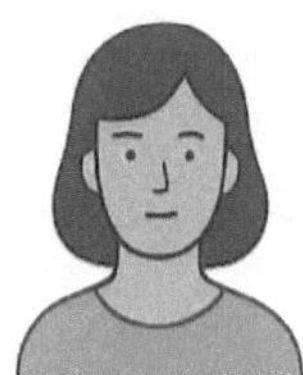

Slow apertures freeze motion but

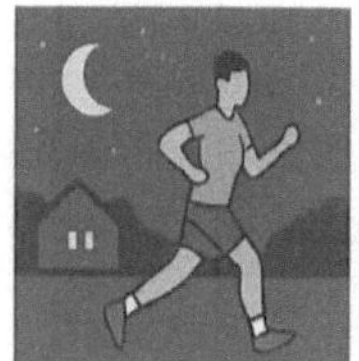

(A) 1/1000

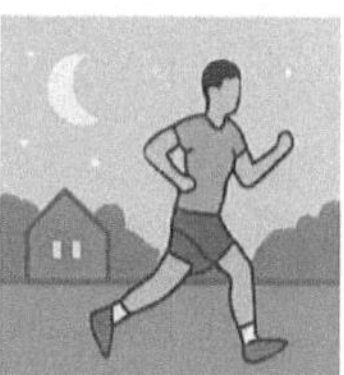

(B) 1/30 sec

Higher ISO brighten the image but adds more digital noise

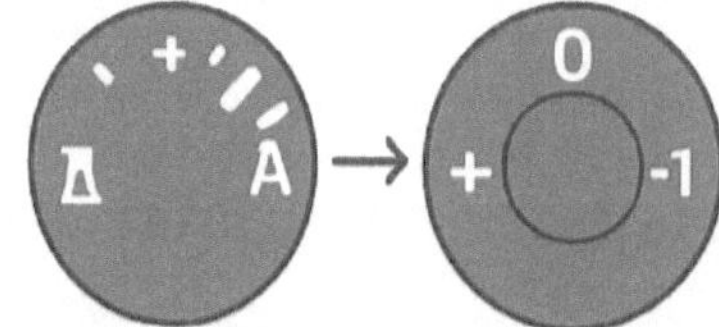

Use exposure compensation to make images brighter (+) or darker (−).

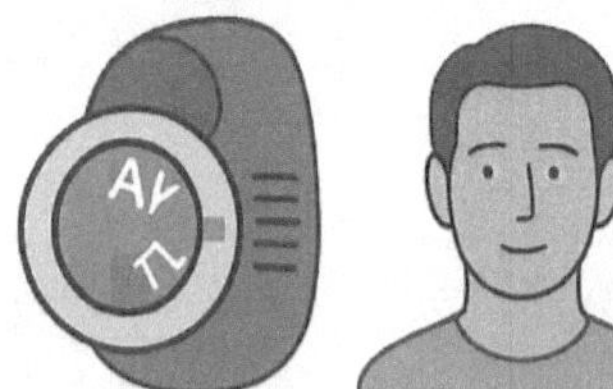

Choose Auto for ease, Av/Tv for balance, or M for full creative control

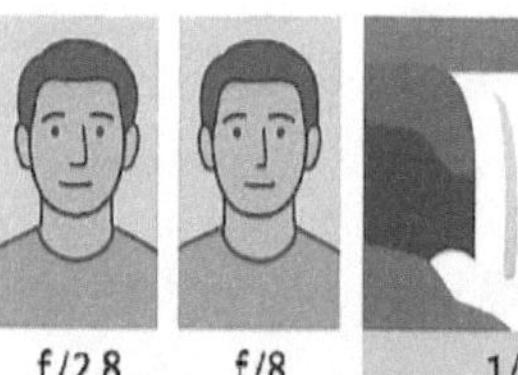

Practice aperture control br photographing the same subject at different f-stops

Chapter 4

Autofocus Mastery: From Blurry to Razor Sharp

Few things frustrate photographers more than a blurry photo. You line up the shot, press the shutter, and instead of a crisp subject, you end up with softness where you wanted sharpness. The Canon EOS R7 is designed to eliminate that frustration. Its Dual Pixel CMOS AF II autofocus system is one of the most advanced on the market, capable of tracking eyes, animals, and fast-moving subjects with breathtaking precision.

But here's the secret: while the camera is incredibly smart, it still needs your guidance. Understanding the autofocus modes and learning when to use them is the difference between random luck and consistent razor-sharp results. In this chapter, we'll explore everything you need to know about autofocus on the R7: from the basics of One Shot vs Servo, to the wonders of face and animal detection, to pro-level tricks like back-button focusing and real-world AF "recipes" for different shooting scenarios.

Introduction to Dual Pixel CMOS AF II

Canon's Dual Pixel CMOS AF II is the heart of the R7's autofocus. Unlike older systems that relied on separate AF sensors, Dual Pixel AF integrates focusing directly into the imaging sensor. Every pixel on the sensor can also act as a focus point, giving the R7 up to 651 automatic AF zones covering nearly 100% of the frame.

What does this mean for you?

- Lightning-fast focus acquisition, even in low light.

- Smooth focus tracking, ideal for both stills and video.

- Intelligent subject recognition: the camera isn't just guessing where to focus; it actually recognizes people, eyes, animals, and vehicles.

Think of Dual Pixel AF II as a second set of eyes that watches your subject as closely as you do — but with superhuman speed.

One Shot vs Servo AF

Your R7 offers two main autofocus modes. Knowing when to use each is essential:

- **One Shot AF:** Focus locks once when you half-press the shutter. Perfect for still subjects like landscapes, posed portraits, or products. Once locked, the focus won't adjust unless you lift your finger and half-press again.
    - *Use when:* Your subject isn't moving.
- **Servo AF:** Continuously adjusts focus as long as you half-press the shutter. Ideal for moving subjects, from kids running to birds flying.
    - *Use when:* Motion is unpredictable and you need constant focus adjustment.

Quick Tip: If you're not sure, Servo is the safer choice — it ensures focus adapts if your subject suddenly moves.

Face, Eye, and Animal Detection

One of the R7's most powerful features is its subject detection system.

- **Face Detection:** Locks onto a human face, even if it's small in the frame.

- **Eye Detection:** Prioritizes the nearest eye — crucial for portraits, since sharp eyes make or break an image.

- **Animal Detection:** Recognizes cats, dogs, and birds. Perfect for pets or wildlife photography.

- **Tracking in Action:** Once detected, the camera keeps locked on the subject even if they move, turn, or momentarily leave the frame.

Example: Photographing your dog running at the park? Switch to Animal Detection with Servo AF. The R7 will track your pet's eyes, even as they dart around unpredictably.

Zone AF vs Single Point: Which to Use When

The R7 offers flexibility in how you choose focus areas:

- **Single Point AF:** You manually place a tiny focus point anywhere in the frame. Extremely precise. Best for still subjects or when you want total control.
  - *Use for:* Macro shots, product photography, or when background clutter might confuse the AF system.

- **Zone AF:** You select a larger zone (like a square or rectangle), and the camera decides what to prioritize within it. Great for moving subjects where exact precision isn't practical.
  - *Use for:* Sports, wildlife, or children where movement is unpredictable.

Rule of Thumb: Single point = control. Zone AF = speed. Choose based on whether your subject is predictable or not.

Back-Button Focus Made Easy

Back-button focusing (BBF) is a pro technique that separates focusing from the shutter button. Instead of half-pressing the shutter to focus, you assign focus to the AF-ON button on the back of the camera. Your thumb controls focus, and your index finger just takes the shot.

Why use BBF?

- Prevents accidental refocusing when you press the shutter.
- Lets you lock focus once, then recompose without losing it.
- In Servo mode, it allows you to track when you want and stop when you don't.

How to set it up:

1. Go to **Menu > AF > AF Operation.**

2. Reassign focus to the AF-ON button in **Custom Controls.**

3. Practice: press AF-ON with your thumb to focus, then press the shutter to shoot.

At first, it feels strange. But once you get used to it, you'll never go back — especially for action or wildlife photography.

Real-Life AF "Recipes"

Here's where it all comes together. These practical autofocus "recipes" show you exactly which settings to use for common scenarios.

1. Portraits

- AF Mode: One Shot

- Detection: Face + Eye

- Focus Area: Single point or small zone

- Tip: Focus on the nearest eye for maximum impact.

2. Moving Kids

- AF Mode: Servo

- Detection: Face + Eye

- Focus Area: Zone AF

- Tip: Keep the child in the zone; the R7 will track automatically.

3. Birds in Flight

- AF Mode: Servo

- Detection: Animal (Birds)

- Focus Area: Wide zone or full area

- Tip: Pan smoothly and let the camera track — it will lock onto the bird's eye if visible.

4. Street Photography

- AF Mode: Servo

- Detection: Face/Eye

- Focus Area: Small zone

- Tip: Set back-button focus so you can lock onto a subject quickly without hunting.

5. Sports Action

- AF Mode: Servo

- Detection: Face/Eye (for people) or Animal (for pets/animals)

- Focus Area: Zone AF

- Tip: Use a faster shutter (1/1000 or faster) to freeze motion.

Closing Thoughts

Autofocus mastery is what transforms your photos from hit-or-miss to consistently sharp. The Canon EOS R7 gives you one of the most intelligent AF systems ever built into a camera — but it's your choices that unlock its true potential.

By learning when to use One Shot vs Servo, how to combine Face/Eye/Animal detection with different AF areas, and embracing back-button focus, you'll no longer worry about blur. Instead, you'll focus — literally and creatively — on capturing the moment as it unfolds.

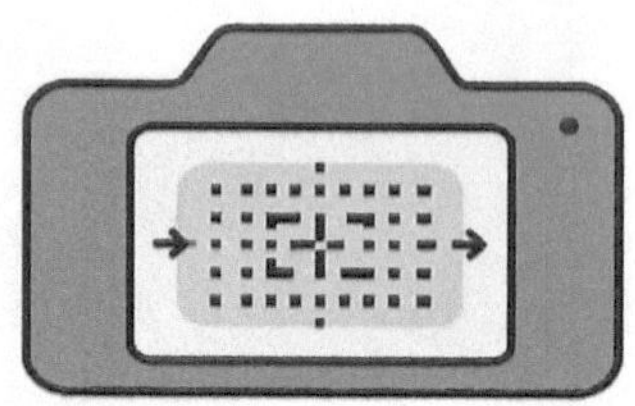

Dual Pixel CMOS AF II uses every pixel on the sensor to achieve fast accurate focus across nearly 100 % of the frame

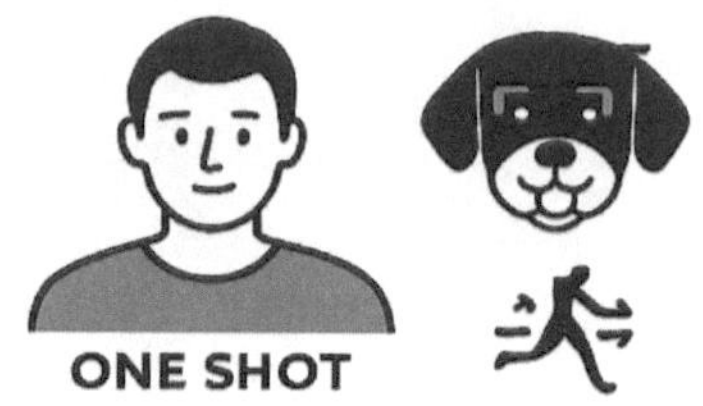

Use One Shot for still subjects and Servo AF for moving subjects.

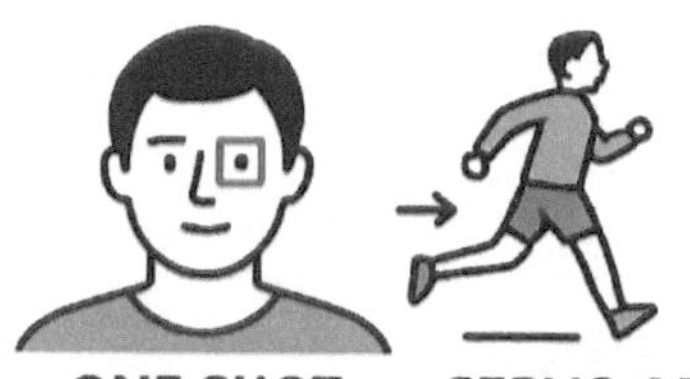

Use One Shot for still subjects and Servo AF for moving subjects

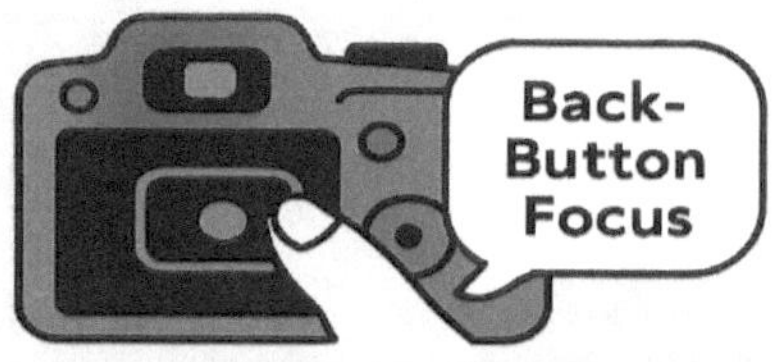

Assign focus to the AF-ON button for faster and more reliable control

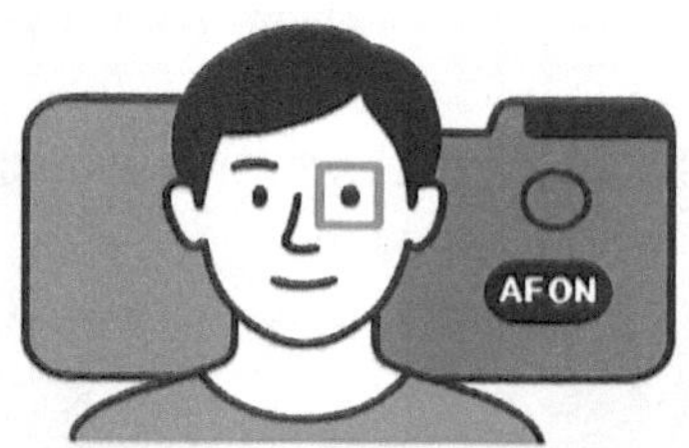

Assign focus to the AF-ON button for faster and more reliable control

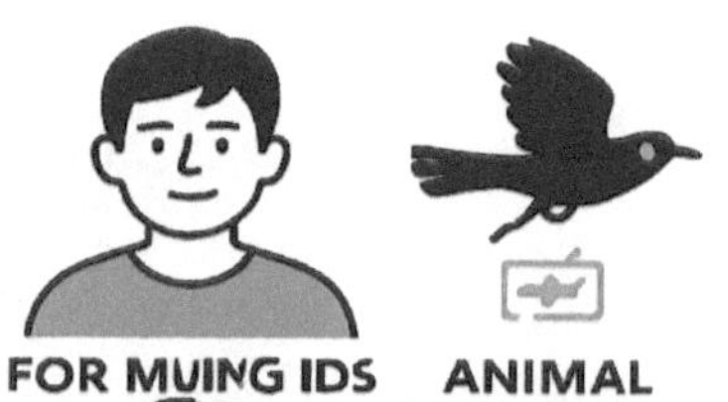

For moving kids: Servo AF with Zone AF and Detection keeps them sharp

FOR PORTRITUSEN:

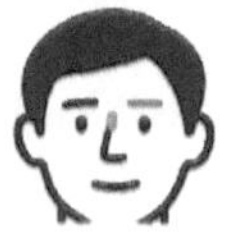
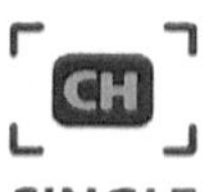

FOR BIRDS IN FLIGHT:

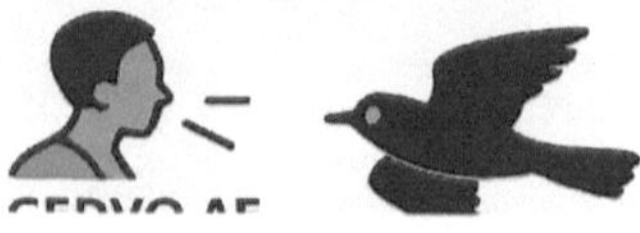

Chapter 5

Shooting Modes & Creative Controls

Every camera is a toolbox, and the Canon EOS R7 offers you a variety of tools to shape your vision. Some of these modes make all the decisions for you, others hand the reins completely over, and some strike a balance in between. Knowing when and how to use them is the difference between letting the camera think for you and using it as an extension of your creativity.

This chapter explores the main shooting modes — from Scene Intelligent Auto to Manual, introduces you to the power of custom modes (C1, C2, C3), explains how to use Picture Styles, and shows you how to make sense of white balance without getting tangled in technical jargon.

By the end, you'll have the confidence to choose modes intentionally instead of relying on luck, and you'll know how to bend the R7's creative controls to match the look and feel you want in your images.

Scene Intelligent Auto vs Creative Auto vs Manual

The EOS R7's mode dial gives you instant access to the camera's personality. Here are the big three approaches:

1. Scene Intelligent Auto (Green "A+" mode):

- The camera makes every decision — aperture, shutter speed, ISO, white balance, and even picture style.

- It's designed for absolute beginners or for moments when you just need a quick snapshot.

- Strength: You can hand the camera to anyone, and it will likely produce a decent photo.

- Limitation: You have almost no control over creative aspects like background blur, motion effects, or color tone.

2. Creative Auto (CA mode):

- A middle ground between Auto and Manual. The camera still handles exposure, but you can tweak effects like background blur (depth of field) and color vibrancy using simple sliders on the touchscreen.

- Great for those who don't want to dive into f-stops and shutter speeds but still want to play with the "look" of their photos.

- Example: Want a soft, dreamy portrait? Use CA mode, slide "background blur" to maximum, and let the camera do the rest.

3. Manual (M mode):

- Full control: you set aperture, shutter speed, and ISO.

- This is where the magic of creativity opens fully — whether you're shooting starry skies, light trails, or carefully composed studio portraits.

- At first, it feels intimidating. But once you understand the exposure triangle (Chapter 3), Manual mode becomes a playground instead of a barrier.

- Example: Photographing fireworks? Set aperture to f/8, shutter to 2 seconds, ISO 100, tripod mounted — all in Manual. The results will amaze you.

Pro Tip: If you're just moving out of Auto, try Av (Aperture Priority) or Tv (Shutter Priority) first. They're not on this outline, but they act as stepping stones toward full Manual control.

Custom Modes (C1, C2, C3) → How to Set Up

On your R7's mode dial, you'll see three custom slots: C1, C2, and C3. These are lifesavers because they allow you to save entire sets of camera settings for instant recall.

Think of them as shortcuts to your favorite setups.

- **C1 Example (Portraits):**

- o Aperture Priority mode (Av), f/2.8 for creamy background blur, Eye Detection ON, Picture Style "Portrait," ISO Auto with max ISO 1600.

- **C2 Example (Wildlife):**

  - o Servo AF, Animal Detection ON, Zone AF, Shutter Priority (Tv) at 1/2000 for freezing motion, ISO Auto max 6400.

- **C3 Example (Video):**

  - o Manual exposure, 4K 60p, shutter at 1/125, aperture f/4, C-Log3 color profile, external mic activated.

How to set them up:

1. Dial in the exact settings you want.

2. Go to Menu > Setup > Custom Shooting Mode (C1–C3).

3. Register the current settings to one of the slots.

4. Now, anytime you twist the dial to C1, C2, or C3, your saved setup is instantly ready.

Pro Tip: Save not just exposure but also autofocus modes, drive modes, and even image formats. It's like programming your camera for different "missions."

Picture Styles and When to Change Them

Picture Styles are like filters built into the camera, but instead of gimmicky effects, they're designed for subtle adjustments to sharpness, contrast, and color.

The R7 offers these defaults:

- **Standard:** Balanced, good for everyday shooting.

- **Portrait:** Softer skin tones, smoother edges.

- **Landscape:** More contrast and vibrant blues/greens.

- **Neutral:** Flatter tones, good for editing later.

- **Faithful:** Accurate color reproduction under daylight.

- **Monochrome:** Black-and-white photography straight out of camera.

When to change Picture Styles:

- Shooting JPEGs → Picture Styles affect the final file.

- Shooting RAW → Styles don't "bake in" but can guide your editing preview.

Example:

- At a wedding → switch to Portrait for flattering skin tones.

- Shooting a mountain vista → try Landscape for richer skies and trees.

- Want artistic B&W → choose Monochrome and preview your scene without distraction.

Pro Tip: Don't overuse Picture Styles. If you plan to edit photos later, stick to Neutral or Standard and do your fine-tuning in software.

White Balance Made Easy

Light has color, even when our eyes don't notice it. White balance (WB) tells the camera what "white" should look like under different lighting. Get it wrong, and your photos may look too orange (warm) or too blue (cool).

The R7 provides presets:

- **Auto WB (AWB):** Camera guesses, usually very good.

- **Daylight:** For shooting in natural sun.

- **Shade:** Warms up images taken in cooler shaded light.

- **Cloudy:** Adds warmth under overcast skies.

- **Tungsten (Incandescent):** Corrects the orange glow of indoor bulbs.

- **Fluorescent:** Neutralizes greenish cast.

- **Custom WB:** You take a photo of a white card and tell the camera, "This is white." Perfect for tricky mixed lighting.

Practical examples:

- Indoors under orange lamps → set Tungsten to balance color.

- Shooting a sunset → use Cloudy to enhance the warm tones instead of neutralizing them.

- Studio work → use Custom WB for consistent color accuracy.

Shortcut: If you're not sure, leave it on AWB. The R7's auto white balance is excellent. But for creative effect, don't be afraid to "break the rules" — warming or cooling your image can add mood.

Closing Thoughts

Shooting modes and creative controls are where the EOS R7 shifts from being just a tool into being your artistic partner. Whether you lean on Auto for simplicity, explore Creative Auto for guided effects, or dive into Manual for complete control, the key is to match the mode to your intention.

By saving setups into custom modes, experimenting with Picture Styles, and mastering white balance, you give yourself the power to adapt instantly and to create images that feel the way you want them to look.

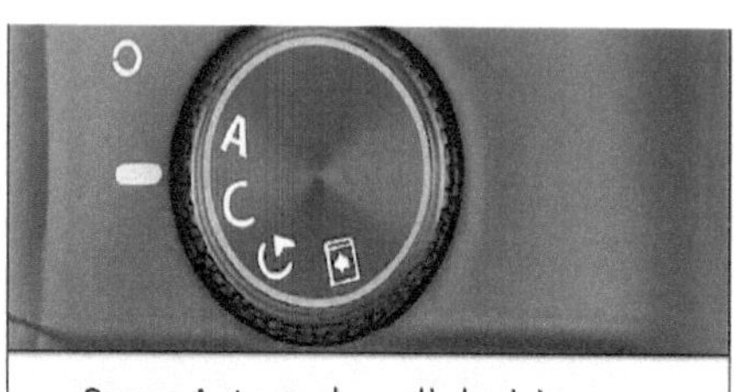

Scene Auto makes all decisions, Creative Auto gives guided control

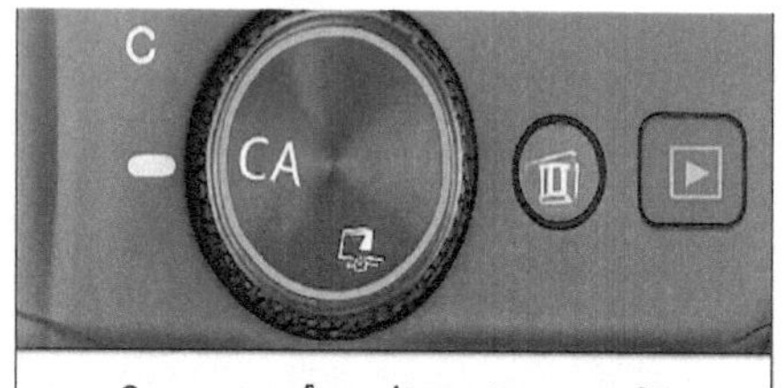

Save your favorite setups, to C1, C2 and C3 for instant recall

Picture Styles

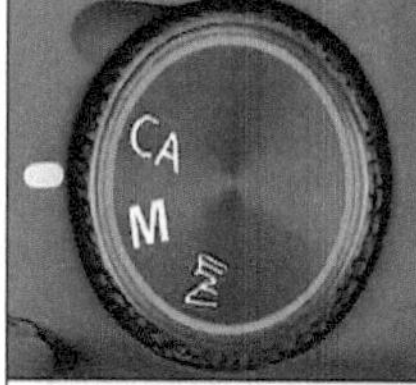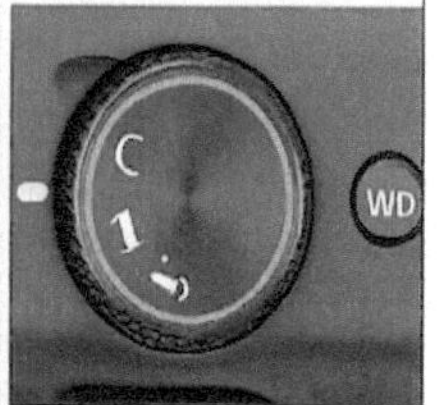

Picture Styles change the look of your images straight out of camera

How to Set a Custom Mode

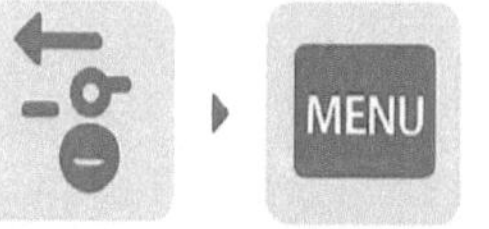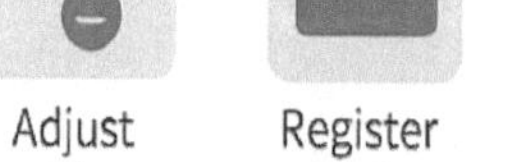

Adjust settings   Register to C1   Register to C1

Dial in your settings, then register them to a custom mode slot

Neutral vs Edited

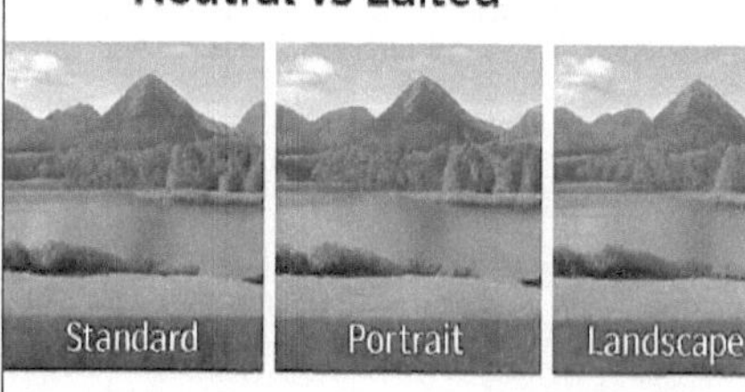

Use Neutral if you plan to edit later; use Standard or Portrait for ready-

White balance Presets

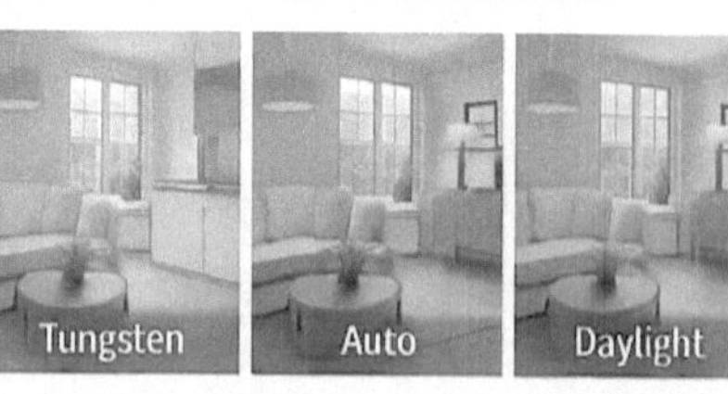

White balance changes how colors appear under different lighting

Chapter 6

Video with the EOS R7

The Canon EOS R7 isn't just a stills powerhouse — it's also one of the most capable video cameras in its class. With its oversampled 4K, slow-motion options, and professional-grade color profiles, it gives you the flexibility to shoot anything from quick YouTube clips to cinematic wedding films. But while the specs sound exciting, the real challenge is knowing which settings to use, when to use them, and how to avoid pitfalls like overheating or poor audio.

This chapter is your roadmap to mastering video on the R7. We'll cover the essential settings, explain advanced features like Canon Log 3, and share practical "recipes" for specific types of projects. By the end, you'll not only understand what the camera can do — you'll know how to set it up for your own creative vision.

Essential Video Settings (Frame Rates,

Resolution, 4K Oversampled)

The R7 gives you multiple video recording modes. Choosing the right one depends on your project.

- **Resolution Options:**

  - **4K Fine (Oversampled):** Records 7K data from the full sensor, downsampled to 4K. This gives incredibly sharp detail with minimal moiré or aliasing. Best choice when quality matters most.

  - **4K Standard:** Regular 4K without oversampling. Slightly less detailed but easier on the processor.

  - **1080p Full HD:** Lower resolution, smaller file sizes, and easier to edit. Good for casual projects or if storage space is limited.

- **Frame Rates:**

  - **24 fps (23.976):** The "cinematic" look. Slight motion blur, perfect for storytelling and films.

-
    - **30 fps:** Smooth but still natural. Great for casual YouTube content or interviews.

    - **60 fps:** Very smooth. Useful for fast action or if you plan to slow footage down later.

    - **120 fps (in 1080p):** Super slow motion (see below).

Pro Tip: If you're unsure, start with 4K Fine at 24 or 30 fps. It balances quality with flexibility.

Recording Slow Motion (1080p/120fps)

Slow motion can transform ordinary clips into dramatic visuals. The R7 makes it easy by offering Full HD at 120 fps.

- **How to set it up:**
    - Go to **Menu > Movie Recording Quality** and select **FHD 119.88 fps**.
    - Note: This disables audio recording — you'll need to add music or narration in editing.

- **Best uses:**

- Sports (a soccer kick, a basketball dunk).

- Nature (birds taking flight, water splashes).

- Emotional moments (a bride tossing flowers, kids playing).

Tip: Slow-motion footage works best with strong light. Shooting indoors at 120 fps may result in noise unless you raise ISO significantly.

C-Log3 vs Standard Profiles

The R7 offers both standard picture profiles and Canon Log 3 (C-Log3), a flat, professional-grade color profile.

- **Standard Profiles (Standard, Neutral, Portrait, Landscape):**

  - Ready-to-use footage, minimal editing needed.

  - Colors look vibrant straight out of the camera.

  - Best for beginners, vloggers, or quick-turnaround projects.

- **Canon Log 3 (C-Log3):**

  - Flat, low-contrast image that preserves highlight and shadow detail.

  - Requires color grading in editing software (Premiere, DaVinci Resolve, Final Cut).

  - Provides more dynamic range and flexibility, closer to a professional cinema camera look.

  - Best for filmmakers or anyone planning to edit seriously.

Rule of Thumb:

- Use Standard if you want fast results with little editing.

- Use C-Log3 if you're aiming for a cinematic look and don't mind post-processing.

Audio Tips: Using External Mics

Even with beautiful footage, poor audio will ruin a video. The EOS R7 has a built-in microphone, but like most cameras, it's only good for scratch audio. For quality sound:

- **External Microphone Options:**
    - **Shotgun Mic (on-camera):** Picks up sound from the front, great for vlogging or interviews.
    - **Lavalier Mic (clip-on):** Small mic clipped to a subject's shirt. Excellent for clean dialogue.
    - **Wireless Systems:** Allow more freedom of movement, perfect for weddings or interviews.
- **Setup Tips:**
    - Plug the mic into the 3.5mm mic input on the camera.
    - Use the headphone jack to monitor audio while recording.
    - Always do a test recording before filming important events.

Pro Tip: Record audio separately on a dedicated recorder as backup during professional shoots. Sync it in editing for best results.

Avoiding Overheating & Best Memory Cards

Recording 4K video pushes the R7's processor hard, so overheating is possible in hot conditions or during long takes.

- **Tips to Prevent Overheating:**
    - Use 4K Standard instead of oversampled Fine for less strain.
    - Avoid leaving the camera in direct sun.
    - Record in shorter bursts instead of one continuous take.
    - Turn off the LCD when not needed, or use the EVF.
- **Best Memory Cards:**
    - The R7 supports UHS-II SD cards. These are essential for smooth 4K 60p or 120 fps recording.

- o Look for V60 or V90 speed class cards to handle high data rates.

- o Example: SanDisk Extreme Pro UHS-II V90 cards are reliable for 4K oversampled and C-Log3 recording.

Warning: Slow cards may stop recording mid-shot, so don't cut corners here.

Real-Life Video "Recipes"

Now let's get practical. Here are setups you can use immediately for different types of projects:

1. YouTube Setup (Vlogging / Tutorials)

- Resolution: 4K Standard at 30 fps.

- Profile: Standard (vibrant, ready-to-go).

- Audio: Shotgun mic on top.

- Lens: Wide-angle (15–35mm equivalent).

- Tip: Use a tripod or handheld gimbal for stability.

2. Wedding Setup

- Resolution: 4K Fine at 24 fps for cinematic detail.

- Profile: C-Log3 (for color grading later).

- Audio: Lavalier mics on groom/officiant, shotgun for ambient.

- Lens: Fast primes (f/1.4–f/2.8) for shallow depth of field.

- Tip: Shoot in bursts and rotate cards often to prevent overheating.

3. Cinematic Look (Short Films / B-Roll)

- Resolution: 4K Fine at 24 fps.

- Profile: C-Log3.

- Shutter Speed: 1/50 sec (for natural motion blur at 24 fps).

- Lenses: Use primes for artistic depth, ND filters outdoors.

- Audio: External recorder with shotgun mic.

- Tip: Color grade in editing to bring out mood and drama.

Closing Thoughts

84

The Canon EOS R7 can adapt to nearly any video project, whether you're uploading a quick vlog or crafting a cinematic masterpiece. By understanding essential settings, experimenting with frame rates, and choosing the right profiles, you unlock its potential as a filmmaking tool. Add external audio, protect against overheating, and practice with the video "recipes" above, and you'll be ready to create content that looks and sounds professional.

4K Fine (Oversampled)

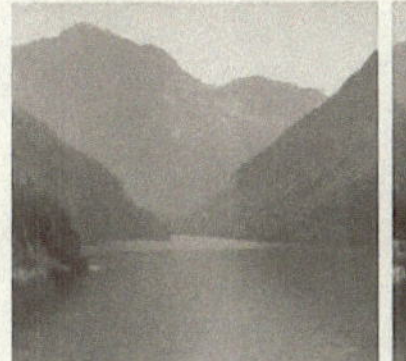 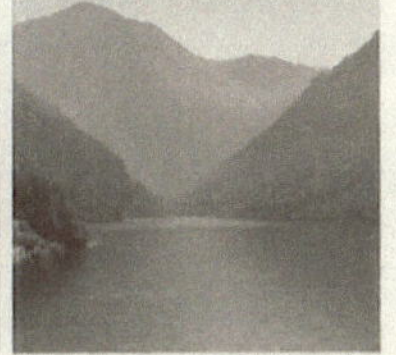

4K Fine   4K Standard

4K Fine (oversampled) delivers maximum detail, while 4K Standard balances quality and efficie-

Slow-Motion

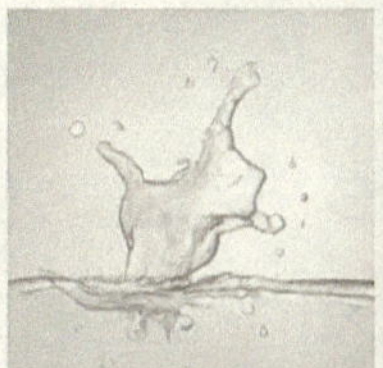 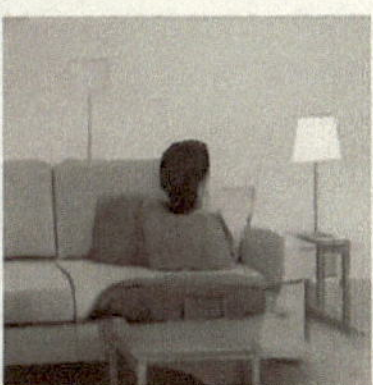

10 min   Standard Profile

Standard gives ready-to-use color, while C-Log3 preserves detail for color grading.

Eus external mics—

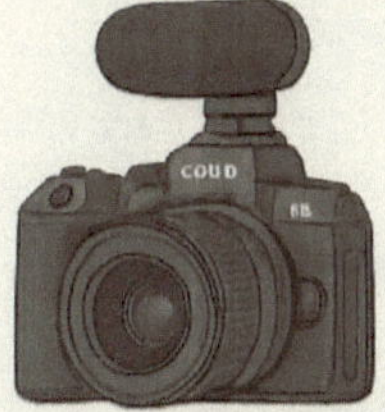 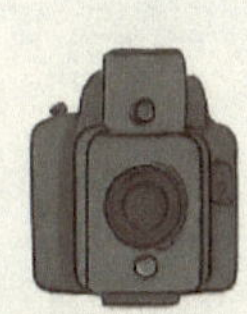

Use external mics—shotgun or lavalier—for clear professional sound.

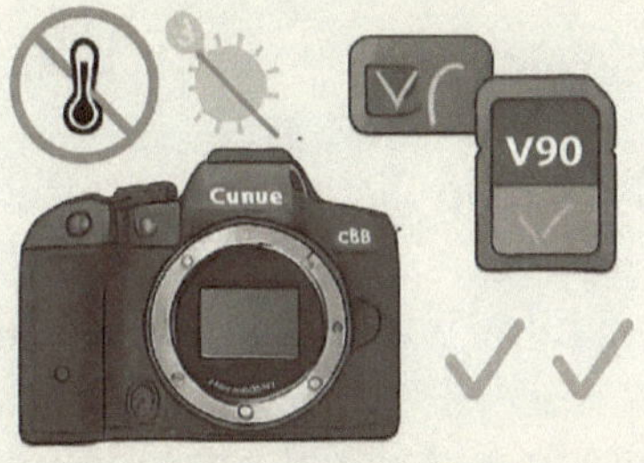

Prevent overheating with short takes and shade, Use fast UHS-ll V60 or V90 cards for reliable 4 reording

YouTube setup:

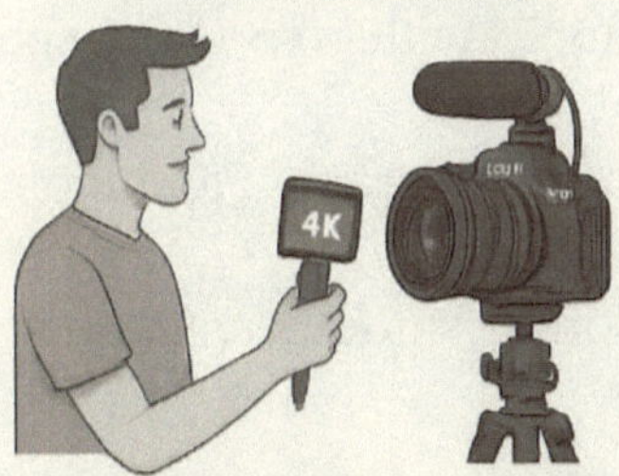

YouTube setup: 4K / 30 fps, Standard profile, wide lens. and shotgun mic

Wedding setup:

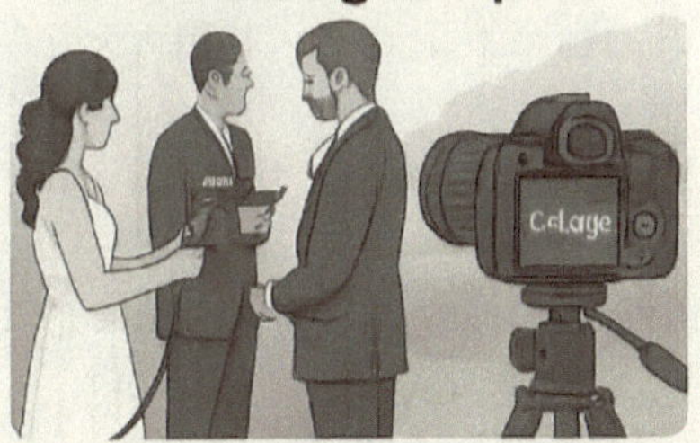

Wedding setup: 4K Fine, C-Log3, fast lenses, and multiple audio sources.

Video recipe: 4 I/ (30 fps, snadimc tuhe stup

Chapter 7

Lenses & Essential Accessories

A camera body is only half the story. What transforms the Canon EOS R7 into a true creative powerhouse is the lens you attach and the accessories you pair it with. The R7's APS-C sensor gives you a 1.6x crop factor, which effectively extends the reach of every lens — a huge advantage for wildlife and sports shooters, but something portrait and travel photographers need to keep in mind.

This chapter will guide you through the best RF-S starter lenses, RF full-frame lenses that pair beautifully with the R7, specific recommendations for different types of photography, and the must-have accessories that make your shooting smoother, sharper, and more enjoyable.

Best RF-S Starter Lenses

Canon designed the RF-S lens lineup specifically for APS-C bodies like the EOS R7. These lenses are lightweight, compact, and budget-friendly.

- **RF-S 18–45mm f/4.5–6.3 IS STM**
    - Often included as a kit lens. Small, collapsible, and portable. Great for casual shooting, family events, and general travel.
    - Strength: Compact and lightweight.
    - Limitation: Narrow aperture (f/4.5–6.3), so less suited for low light or creamy background blur.
- **RF-S 18–150mm f/3.5–6.3 IS STM**
    - A versatile "all-in-one" zoom. Covers wide-angle to telephoto, making it perfect for travel, landscapes, and casual wildlife shooting.
    - Strength: Excellent range.
    - Limitation: Narrow aperture at the long end.

Tip: If you're starting from scratch, the 18–150mm is the best single-lens solution for flexibility.

RF Full-Frame Lenses That Work Beautifully on the R7

One of the R7's strengths is its ability to use Canon's full-frame RF lenses seamlessly. Thanks to the crop factor, many lenses effectively give you extra reach, which is perfect for telephoto needs.

- **RF 50mm f/1.8 STM ("Nifty Fifty")**
    - Affordable prime lens. On the R7, it behaves like an 80mm — perfect for portraits.
    - Wide f/1.8 aperture allows shallow depth of field and low-light shooting.
- **RF 24–105mm f/4L IS USM**
    - Professional-quality zoom with stabilization. On the R7, it becomes roughly 38–168mm. Great for travel, events, and portraits.

- **RF 70–200mm f/4L IS USM**

  - o On the R7, effectively 112–320mm. Ideal for wildlife, sports, and distant subjects. Compact compared to older 70–200 designs.

- **RF 100–500mm f/4.5–7.1L IS USM**

  - o A dream telephoto lens. On the R7, you get 160–800mm reach — perfect for birders and wildlife enthusiasts.

Pro Insight: Full-frame primes and L-series zooms will give you the sharpest results, but they're also more expensive.

Recommended Lenses by Genre

Different styles of photography benefit from specific focal lengths and lens types. Here are practical recommendations:

- **Portraits:**

  - o RF 50mm f/1.8 STM (budget option).

- RF 85mm f/2 Macro IS STM (for flattering portraits with beautiful background blur).

    - RF 24–70mm f/2.8L IS USM (professional versatility).

- **Travel:**

    - RF-S 18–150mm f/3.5–6.3 IS STM (all-in-one convenience).

    - RF 24–105mm f/4L IS USM (better optics, more professional feel).

    - RF 35mm f/1.8 Macro IS STM (lightweight prime, great for food and street).

- **Landscapes:**

    - RF 16mm f/2.8 STM (super wide, affordable).

    - RF 15–35mm f/2.8L IS USM (professional wide zoom with sharpness and speed).

    - RF-S 18–45mm f/4.5–6.3 IS STM (starter wide-angle option).

- **Wildlife:**

o   RF 100–400mm f/5.6–8 IS USM (budget telephoto).

o   RF 100–500mm f/4.5–7.1L IS USM (pro wildlife lens).

o   Pair with the R7 crop factor for stunning long reach.

Must-Have Accessories

The right accessories make a big difference in both convenience and image quality. Here are essentials every R7 user should consider:

- **Tripod:**

  o   For landscapes, long exposures, video, or astrophotography. Look for sturdy but lightweight carbon fiber options if you travel often.

- **Flashes (Speedlites):**

  o   Canon Speedlite EL-100 or EL-1. Use for portraits, events, or low light when natural light isn't enough. Off-camera flashes add creative lighting control.

- **ND Filters (Neutral Density):**

- o Reduce light entering the lens. Essential for video (to keep natural shutter speeds in bright light) or long-exposure photography (silky waterfalls, smooth skies).

- **Extra Batteries:**

  - o The R7 uses LP-E6NH batteries. Video recording, burst shooting, and long days outdoors drain power fast. Always carry spares.

- **External Microphones:**

  - o For video, upgrade from the built-in mic. Shotgun mics capture directional sound; lavaliers capture dialogue. Clean audio is as important as sharp video.

- **Memory Cards:**

  - o Invest in UHS-II V60 or V90 cards for smooth 4K video and burst photography. Slow cards may buffer or fail mid-recording.

Practical Note: Start with the basics (tripod, spare battery, fast SD card) and add accessories as your needs grow.

Closing Thoughts

The Canon EOS R7 is versatile enough to handle any subject, but lenses and accessories are what unlock its full potential. Whether you want to capture the shimmer in a bride's eyes, the sweep of a mountain vista, or a hawk soaring overhead, the right glass and gear make all the difference.

Invest wisely — choose one or two lenses that match your favorite subjects, and build your kit from there. With thoughtful accessories, you'll spend less time wrestling with limitations and more time focusing on creativity.

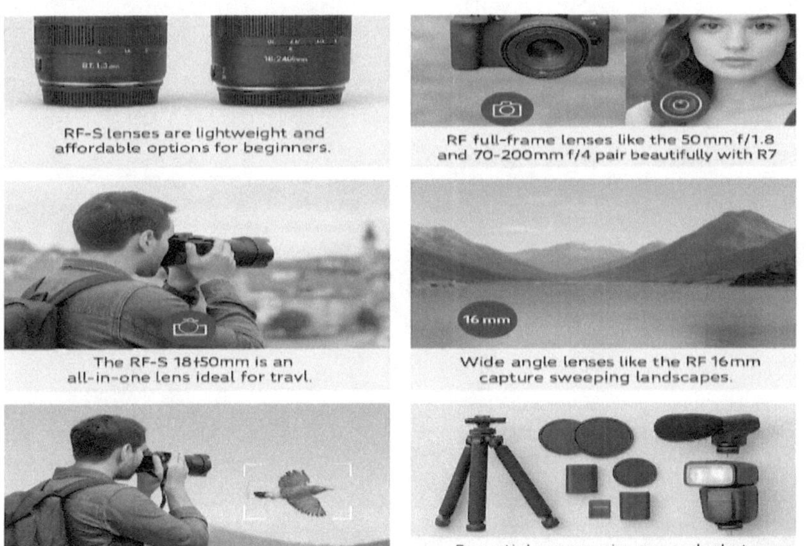

Chapter 8

Real-Life Shooting Recipes

Knowing the technical side of your EOS R7 is one thing. Putting it into practice is another. Real creativity comes alive when you use your camera in the real world: capturing your family in natural light, freezing the action of your kids' soccer game, or pointing your lens at the night sky.

This chapter is designed as your cookbook for photography. Each scenario is a "recipe" with clear steps, recommended settings, and pro tips. You can try them right away, then adapt them to your style as you grow more confident.

Family Portraits at Home

There's no better subject than the people closest to you. The R7 excels at portraits thanks to its face and eye detection autofocus.

Settings Recipe:

- Mode: Av (Aperture Priority)

- Aperture: f/2.8 – f/4 (blurs the background, keeps eyes sharp).

- ISO: Auto, max 1600.

- White Balance: Auto indoors; adjust if light looks too warm/cool.

- Autofocus: One Shot AF, Eye Detection ON.

Tips:

- Position subjects near a window for natural, flattering light.

- Use the RF 50mm f/1.8 STM or RF 85mm f/2 for creamy background blur.

- Avoid cluttered backgrounds; use a neutral wall or simple props.

- Encourage natural interaction — laughter and movement bring photos to life.

Wildlife Photography at the Park

Birds, squirrels, or even your dog running free — the R7's crop factor makes it a fantastic wildlife camera.

Settings Recipe:

- Mode: Tv (Shutter Priority)

- Shutter Speed: 1/2000 sec (to freeze motion).

- Aperture: Camera auto-sets.

- ISO: Auto, max 6400.

- Autofocus: Servo AF, Animal Detection ON, Zone AF.

Tips:

- Use telephoto lenses (100–400mm, 100–500mm).

- Shoot in bursts to increase chances of capturing the perfect wing position.

- Anticipate behavior: focus where the animal is going, not just where it is.

- Patience is your greatest accessory.

Travel & Street Photography

Travel and street shooting are about storytelling — capturing atmosphere, details, and fleeting moments.

Settings Recipe:

- Mode: Av (Aperture Priority)

- Aperture: f/5.6 – f/8 (balance subject and environment).

- ISO: Auto, max 3200.

- White Balance: Auto or Shade for warmth.

- Autofocus: Servo AF, Face + Eye Detection, or small Zone.

Tips:

- Use a versatile lens like RF-S 18–150mm or RF 24–105mm.

- Be discreet: use the vari-angle screen to shoot from the hip.

- Capture details (doors, food, hands) along with wide cityscapes.

- Look for light and shadow play in urban settings for dramatic compositions.

Landscapes at Sunrise/Sunset

Golden hour is the most rewarding time to photograph nature.

Settings Recipe:

- Mode: Av (Aperture Priority)

- Aperture: f/8 – f/11 (maximize sharpness and depth).

- ISO: 100–200.

- Autofocus: One Shot, Single Point.

- White Balance: Cloudy to enhance warm tones.

- Tripod recommended.

Tips:

- Arrive early and scout your location.

- Use wide lenses (16mm, 18mm).

- Include foreground interest (rocks, flowers, water) for depth.

- Bracket exposures (+/- 1 stop) to balance highlights and shadows.

Sports & Action Shots

The R7's fast autofocus and 30 fps burst mode make it a sports beast.

Settings Recipe:

- Mode: Tv (Shutter Priority)

- Shutter Speed: 1/1000 sec or faster.

- ISO: Auto, max 6400.

- Autofocus: Servo AF, Face/Eye Detection ON, Zone AF.

- Drive: High-speed continuous.

Tips:

- Anticipate peak action — the kick, the jump, the swing.

- Use telephoto lenses (70–200mm, 100–400mm).

- Keep both eyes open to track movement outside your frame.

- Burst mode helps — but don't just "spray and pray"; time your shots.

Vlogging / Content Creation Setup

The R7 doubles as an excellent content creation tool with 4K video and a flip-out screen.

Settings Recipe:

- Mode: Movie (Video).

- Resolution: 4K 30 fps (Standard).

- Picture Style: Standard for quick editing, C-Log3 if grading.

- Audio: Shotgun mic on top **or** lavalier mic.

- Lens: Wide-angle (16mm, 18mm).

Tips:

- Frame yourself using the vari-angle screen.

- Use a tripod, gimbal, or handheld grip for stability.

- Add an ND filter outdoors for natural shutter speeds.

- Speak close to the mic for best sound clarity.

Night Sky & Long Exposures

Astrophotography is where the R7 truly shines with clean, detailed images.

Settings Recipe:

- Mode: M (Manual).

- Aperture: Wide open (f/2.8 or lower).

- Shutter: 20 seconds (to avoid star trails).

- ISO: 1600–3200.

- Focus: Manual, set to infinity.

- Tripod essential.

Tips:

- Use a wide fast lens (16mm f/2.8, 24mm f/1.4).

- Enable 2-second self-timer or remote shutter to avoid shake.

- Shoot RAW for flexibility in editing.

- Scout a location far from city lights.

Closing Thoughts

These recipes are designed to get you shooting right away. As you practice, you'll start tweaking settings to match your vision. That's the beauty of photography — no two recipes ever look exactly alike. The EOS R7 is built to handle all of it: quiet family portraits, breathtaking wildlife, bustling city scenes, and even the stars above.

Experiment, adjust, and most importantly — enjoy the process. The more you practice, the more natural these setups will become, until you're capturing sharp, expressive images without even thinking about settings.

Real-Life Shooting Recipies

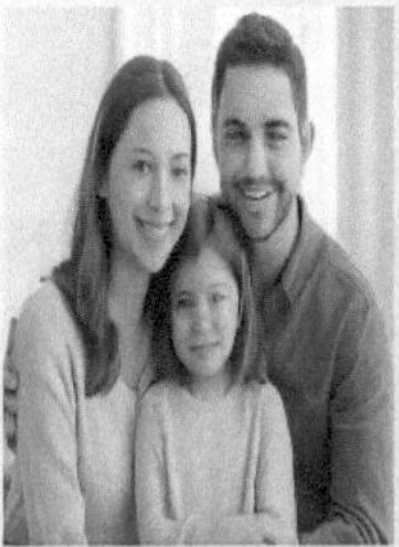 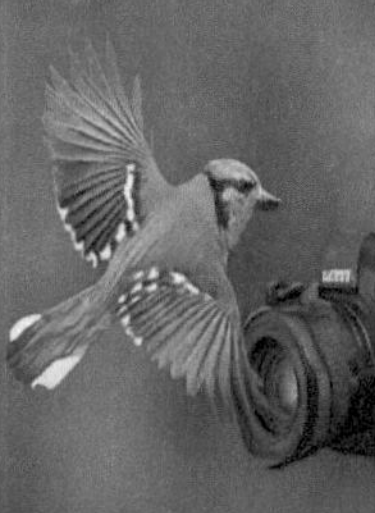 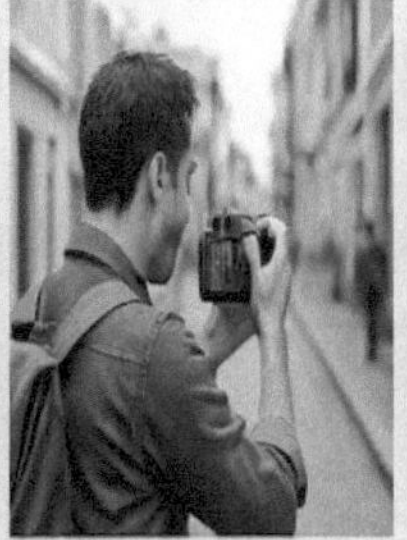 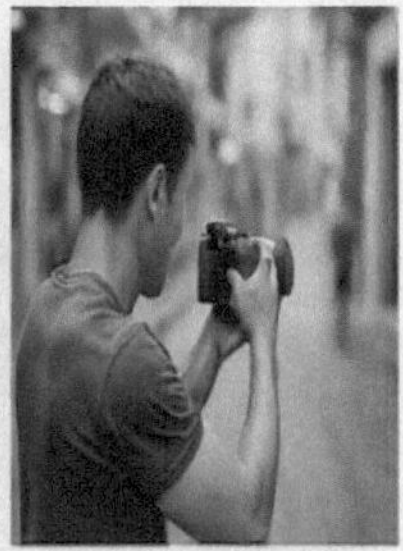

Family Portrait at Home
Family portraits shine with soft window light and Eve Detection AF

Wildlife at the Park
Use Servo AF with telephoto lenses to track wildlife in motion

Travel & Street Photography
Versatile zoom lenses make street and travel 'photography

Sports & Action
Fast shutter speeds and Servo AF freeze the peak an

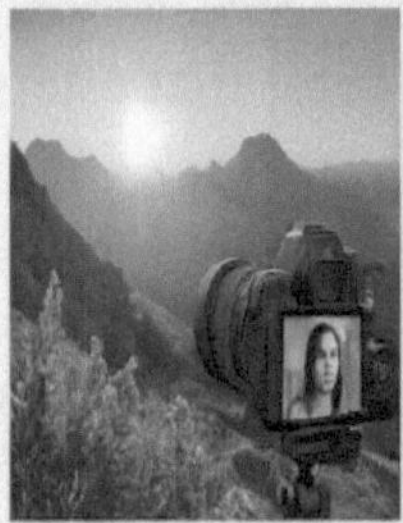 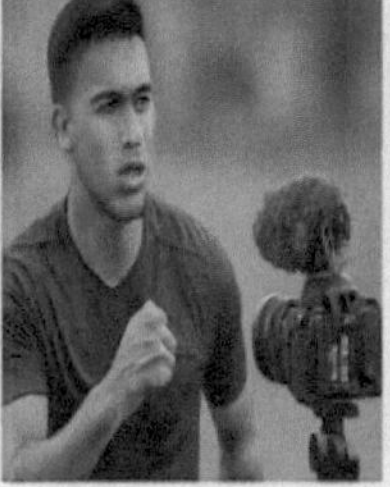 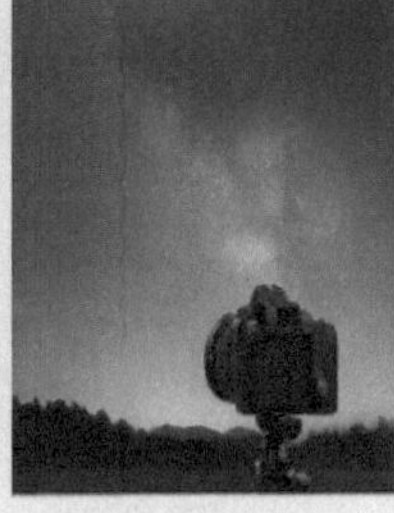 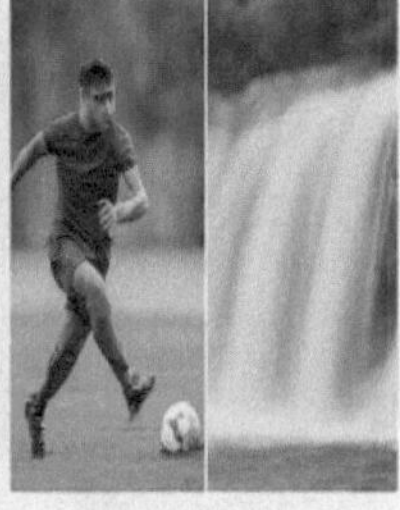

Landscape at Sunrise
At sunrise, use f/3 - f/11 for sharp, detailed landscapes

Sports & Action'
Far vlogs, use 4K video, a wide lens, and an external mic

Night Sky Photography
Manual mode with 20 second exposures reveals night sky intal

Long Exposure Examplie
Experiment with long exposures for creative effects at night-or w

Chapter 9

Advanced Tips & Hidden Features

By now, you've learned how to take sharp photos, shoot in creative modes, and even record professional-quality video. But the EOS R7 holds even more power beneath the surface — features that often go unnoticed, yet can transform how you shoot. These advanced tools aren't just for professionals; they're shortcuts, efficiency boosters, and creative unlocks for anyone willing to explore.

In this chapter, we'll dive into HDR shooting, exposure bracketing, multiple exposures, interval timers, focus aids like peaking and zebras, the digital teleconverter, and workflow tips that make the R7 an even faster, smarter partner.

HDR Mode, Bracketing, and Multiple

Exposures

HDR Mode (High Dynamic Range):

- The R7 can automatically merge multiple exposures into one, balancing bright highlights and dark shadows.

- Perfect for high-contrast scenes like sunsets or interiors with bright windows.

- Found in the Shooting Menu > HDR PQ Settings.

- You'll get a more balanced JPEG file without heavy editing.

Exposure Bracketing:

- Bracketing captures multiple versions of the same photo at different exposures (e.g., −1, 0, +1 EV).

- Useful for blending later in editing, or just ensuring you "nail it" in tricky lighting.

- Set in Menu > Exposure Comp./AEB Setting.

- Example: Photographing a snowy landscape where the camera might underexpose — bracketing ensures you capture safe, bright, and dark versions.

Multiple Exposures:

- A creative feature that lets you layer two or more images into one.

- Example: A portrait overlaid with a city skyline or texture.

- Found in Menu > Multiple Exposure.

- Fun for artistic experiments — but remember, it works best with strong silhouettes or patterns.

Tip: Always use a tripod for HDR and bracketing to keep alignment consistent.

Interval Timer & Time-Lapse

The EOS R7 makes it easy to create cinematic time-lapse sequences without special gear.

Interval Timer:

- Automatically shoots photos at set intervals.

- Example: One shot every 10 seconds for an hour = 360 photos, which can later be stitched into a time-lapse in editing software.

- Menu: Shooting Menu > Interval Timer.

In-Camera Time-Lapse Movie:

- Instead of stitching yourself, the R7 can assemble a time-lapse movie automatically.

- Example: Clouds rolling over mountains, city traffic trails, or flowers opening.

- Menu: Movie Shooting Menu > Time-Lapse Movie.

Pro Tip: Use a tripod, low ISO, and manual focus. Plan your interval — shorter intervals for fast motion (cars), longer intervals for slow changes (sunset).

Using Focus Peaking & Zebras

These tools are essential for manual focus and exposure confidence:

Focus Peaking:

- Outlines the edges of in-focus areas with a bright color (red, blue, or yellow).

- Perfect for macro work, product shots, or manual-focus lenses.

- Enable in Menu > MF Peaking Settings.

Zebras:

- Overlays diagonal stripes on areas of the image that are overexposed (too bright).

- A lifesaver when shooting video, preventing blown-out highlights.

- Enable in Menu > Zebra Display.

- Example: Recording an interview near a window — zebras warn you if the subject's face is too bright.

Workflow Trick: Use zebras to expose for skin tones at around 70% brightness.

Digital Teleconverter Tricks

The EOS R7 offers a Digital Teleconverter (1.6x or 2x crop applied digitally). While it reduces resolution, it can be handy:

- **When to Use:**
  - Wildlife or sports when your lens just isn't long enough.
  - Quick social media posts where you don't need maximum resolution.
- **Where to Find: Menu > Digital Teleconverter.**

Example: With the RF 100–400mm lens, activating 2x teleconverter effectively gives you an 800mm view — great for distant birds without carrying heavy glass.

Note: For best quality, use the teleconverter only in bright light to minimize noise in cropped files.

Tips for Speed & Workflow Efficiency

Advanced cameras like the R7 can overwhelm with menus and options. These tips streamline your shooting:

1. **Customize Buttons & My Menu:**
   - Assign ISO to the M-Fn button, AF area to the joystick press, and register your most-used features (format card, interval timer, custom WB) in the green *My Menu* tab.

2. **Use Custom Modes (C1, C2, C3):**
   - Already covered earlier, but worth repeating: pre-program setups for portraits, wildlife, or video.

3. **Use Touchscreen Shortcuts:**

   o Tap to change ISO, shutter, and aperture instantly instead of scrolling dials.

4. **Dual Card Slots = Safety:**

   o Use **Simultaneous Recording** for automatic backups of important shoots.

5. **Set Auto ISO Limits:**

   o In **ISO settings**, define max ISO (like 6400) to prevent noisy surprises.

6. **Silent Shutter Mode:**

   o Perfect for weddings, wildlife, or street scenes where discretion matters.

7. **Rating & Protecting Images in Camera:**

   o While reviewing, you can add star ratings or lock important shots — making it easier to organize later.

Efficiency Secret: Spend 10 minutes customizing your R7, and you'll save hours of frustration in the field.

Closing Thoughts

The EOS R7 is more than just menus and megapixels — it's a camera designed to work with you. Advanced features like HDR, focus peaking, zebras, and custom workflows elevate your photography from competent to confident. By using these tools intentionally, you'll shoot smarter, faster, and with more creative freedom.

This chapter is your invitation to dig deeper. Try HDR landscapes, experiment with multiple exposures, shoot your first time-lapse, or push your telephoto reach with the digital converter. Each feature is a stepping stone to making the EOS R7 feel like an extension of your vision.

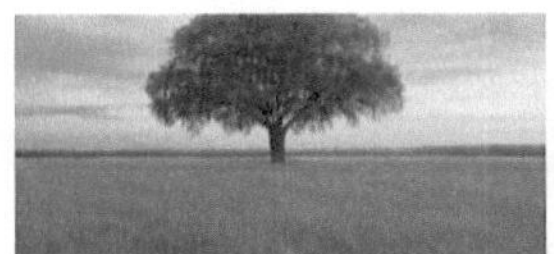

HDR blends multiple
exposures for balanced clet

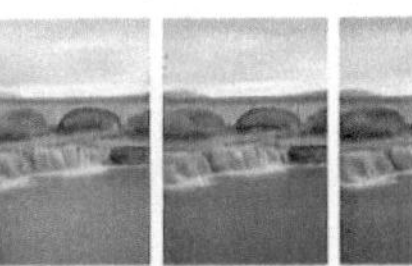

Bracketing ensures you
capture the right exposure
in tricky light

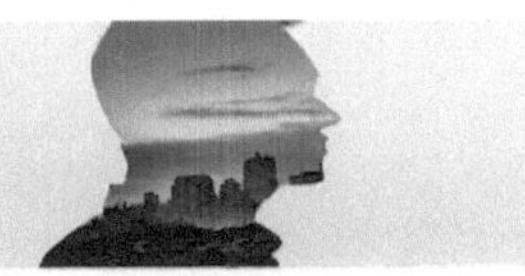

Multiple exposures allow
creative blends in-camara

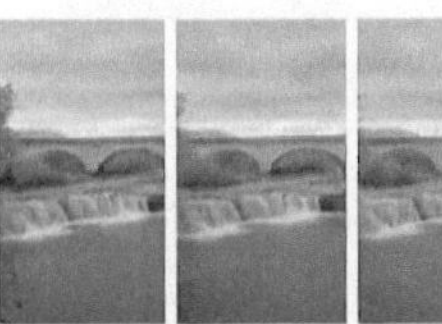

The interval timer makes
time-lapse easy withut
extra gear

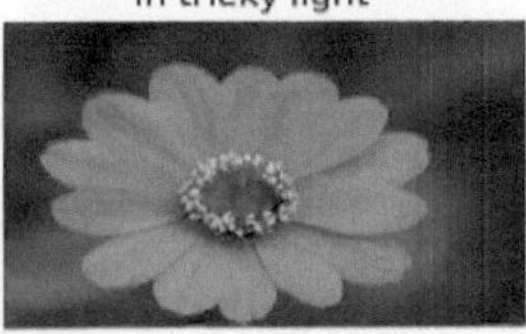

Focus peaking shows
exactly what's sharp in
manual focus

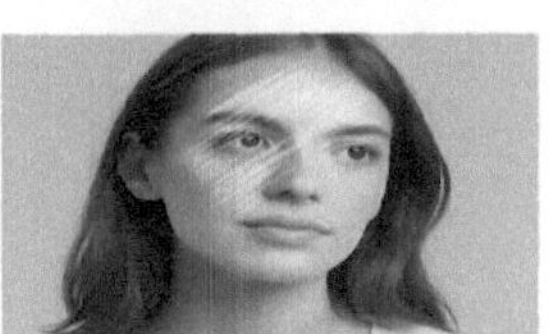

Zebras warn you when
highlights ars too bright

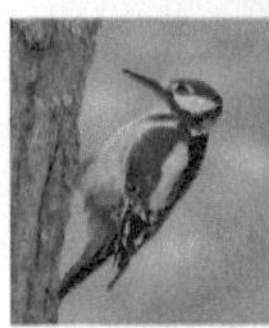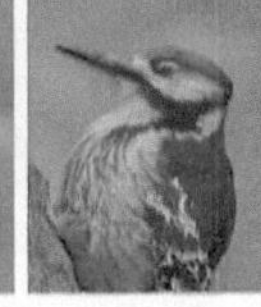

The digital teleconverter
extends reach without

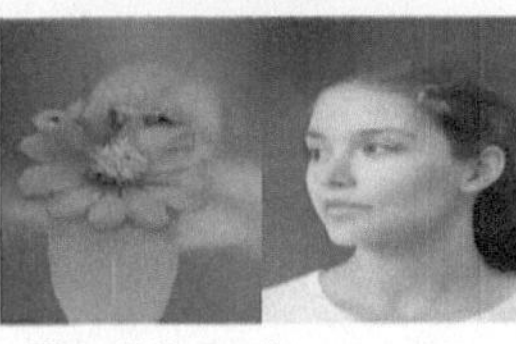

The digital teleconverter
extends reach without

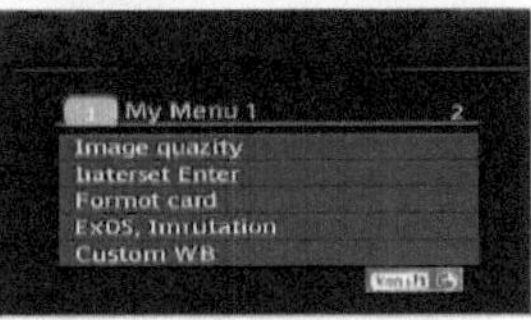

Custemize My Menu and
butteris to speed up

Chapter 10

Troubleshooting & Quick Fixes

Every photographer eventually runs into problems — blurry shots, strange error messages, or a camera that won't last through the day. The good news? With the EOS R7, most issues are simple to fix once you know where to look.

This chapter gives you a practical troubleshooting toolkit. Each section addresses a common problem, explains the cause, and walks you through quick fixes so you can get back to shooting without stress.

Blurry Photos (AF Issues & Fixes)

Few things are more frustrating than a soft image. Before you blame the camera, check these common causes:

1. Wrong Autofocus Mode

- If your subject is moving, using One Shot AF will cause blur. Switch to Servo AF to track motion.

- For portraits, enable Eye Detection AF for sharper eyes.

2. Shutter Speed Too Slow

- Rule of thumb: keep shutter speed at least 1/focal length (e.g., 1/200 sec for a 200mm lens).

- For sports or wildlife, use 1/1000 sec or faster.

3. Camera Shake

- Use Image Stabilization (IS) if your lens supports it.

- Increase ISO to allow faster shutter speeds.

- Consider a tripod or monopod.

Quick Fix Checklist:

- Switch to Servo AF for moving subjects.

- Raise shutter speed.

- Enable Eye/Face Detection.

- Use burst mode to increase keeper rate.

Low Light Noise Solutions

Shooting in dim light often produces noisy, grainy images. Here's how to reduce it:

1. Keep ISO in Check

- The R7 handles ISO up to about 3200 well. Beyond that, noise increases.
- Use Auto ISO with a max limit set (Menu > ISO Settings > Max ISO).

2. Open the Aperture

- Wide apertures (f/1.8, f/2.8) let in more light, reducing the need for high ISO.

3. Slow the Shutter (with Care)

- If your subject isn't moving, use a tripod and longer shutter speeds to gather light instead of raising ISO.

4. Use Noise Reduction in Camera or Post

- Enable High ISO Noise Reduction in the R7's menu for JPEGs.

- For RAW files, use Lightroom/other software for more control.

Pro Tip: Shoot RAW in low light — noise cleans up better in editing than in-camera.

Buffer and Lag Problems

When shooting bursts, especially in RAW, you may hit the R7's buffer limit, causing lag.

Fixes:

1. **Use UHS-II SD Cards** — slower cards choke the buffer. Choose V60 or V90 rated cards.

2. **Switch to JPEG or RAW+HEIF** if you don't need full RAW for every shot.

3. **Shoot in Controlled Bursts** — avoid holding the shutter continuously; release and resume to let the buffer clear.

4. **Reduce Continuous AF Features** if not necessary, as they can slow processing slightly.

Fixing Memory Card Errors

Sometimes the R7 displays card errors or refuses to save files. Don't panic.

Step 1: Remove and Reinsert the Card

- Power off, remove card, reinsert carefully.

Step 2: Format the Card in Camera

- Menu > Setup > Format Card. Always format cards in the camera you're using.

Step 3: Try a Second Card

- If the error persists, test another card.

Step 4: Replace Faulty Cards

- Cards do wear out. Stick to reputable brands (SanDisk, Lexar, ProGrade).

Warning: Never delete files from the card on your computer. Always format in-camera to maintain stability.

Battery Saving Hacks

Mirrorless cameras consume more power than DSLRs, but smart habits extend battery life:

1. **Turn Off the LCD When Possible** — use the EVF to save power.

2. **Enable Eco Mode** — found in Setup Menu, reduces screen brightness and activity.

3. **Limit Burst Shooting & 4K Video** — they drain batteries faster.

4. **Carry Spares (LP-E6NH)** — always have at least two extras for long days.

5. **Use Airplane Mode** — disable Wi-Fi/Bluetooth when not transferring files.

6. **Lower Screen Brightness** indoors.

Tip: Don't store batteries fully drained or fully charged for long periods — keep them at ~60% for storage.

Resetting the Camera Without Panic

Sometimes, after experimenting with settings, your camera may behave oddly. Instead of worrying, reset calmly:

1. Reset Menus:

- Menu > Setup > Reset Camera.

- This resets shooting settings, menus, and custom functions, but keeps firmware updates.

2. Partial Reset:

- You can reset only exposure, network, or custom functions individually.

3. Save Custom Presets:

- Before resetting, save favorite setups in C1–C3 modes so you don't lose them.

Pro Tip: A reset isn't a failure — it's like rebooting a computer. Use it if the camera feels sluggish, menus look strange, or you've changed too much at once.

Closing Thoughts

Troubleshooting is part of every photographer's journey. The difference between frustration and confidence lies in knowing quick fixes. With the EOS R7, most problems come down to simple solutions: switching AF modes, formatting a card, or carrying an extra battery.

Think of this chapter as your safety net. The next time you see blur, noise, or an error message, you'll have a calm checklist to run through. Instead of panic, you'll feel prepared — and ready to get back to capturing the moments that matter.

Blurry Photos Fix

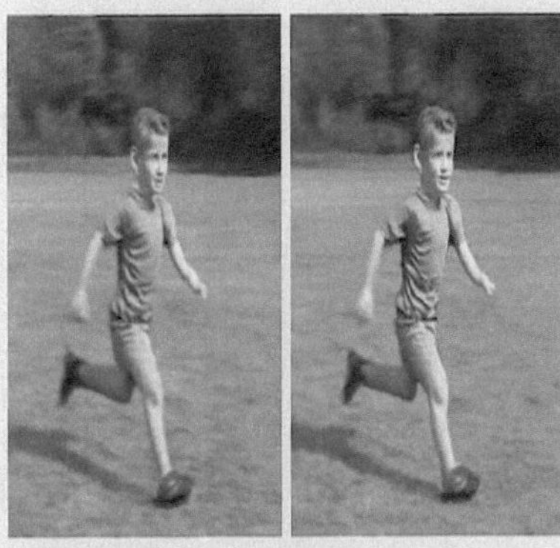

Switch **to Servo AF** for moving
subjects to keep them sharp.

Low Light Noise

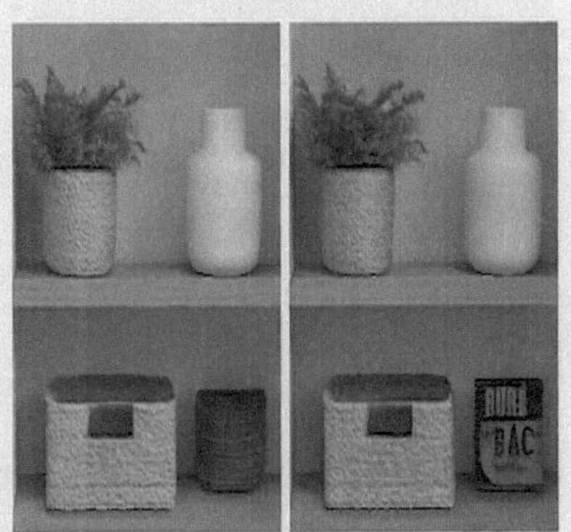

Use wide apertures and lower ISO
to reduce noise in low light

Buffer & Lag

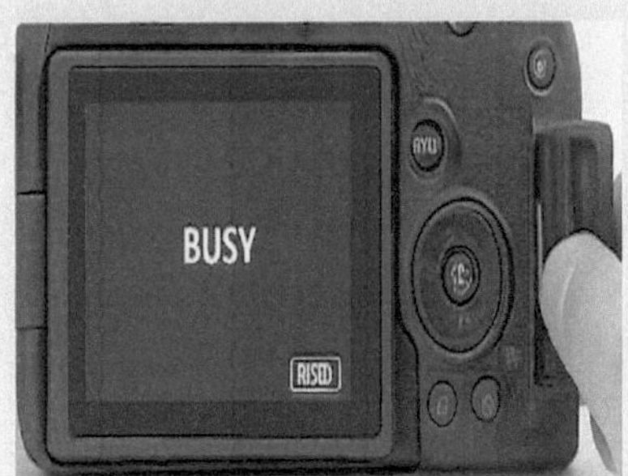

Fast UHS-II cards prevent buffer
slowdowns during bursts

Memory Card Errors

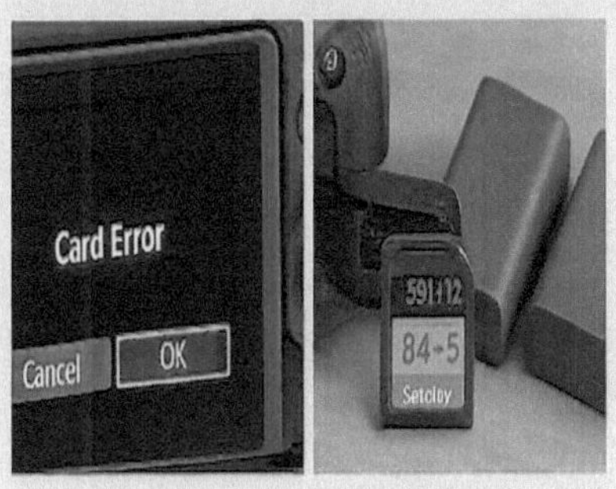

Reinsert or reformat the card
in-camera to fix errors

Battery Saving

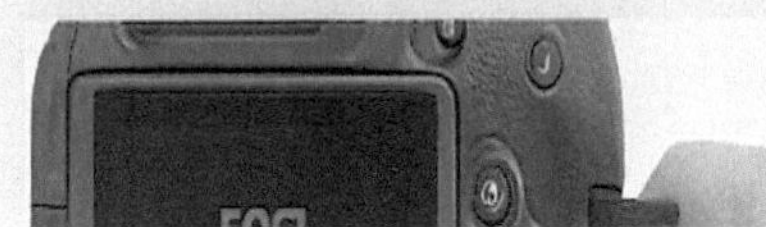

Resetting the Camera

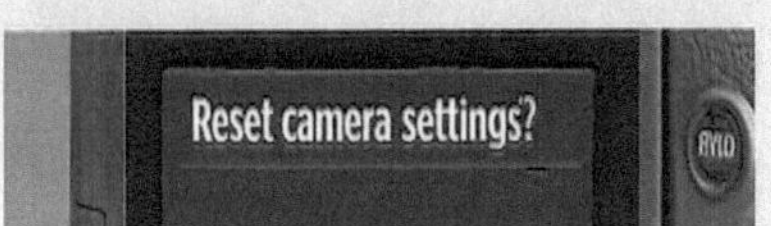

Chapter 11

Quick Reference Cheat Sheets

Sometimes you don't have time to dive into menus or recall full explanations. That's where cheat sheets come in — quick guides you can glance at to remind yourself of the essentials. These pages summarize the most important settings and choices for shooting with the Canon EOS R7.

ISO / Exposure Cheat Sheet

ISO Guidelines

- ISO 100–400 → Bright daylight (cleanest results).

- ISO 800–1600 → Indoors, evening, dim light.

- ISO 3200–6400 → Low light or action at night (some noise).

- ISO 6400+ → Extreme low light (last resort).

Shutter Speed Rules

- 1/60 → Minimum handheld for wide lenses.

- 1/200 → Freeze portraits and everyday motion.

- 1/1000 → Sports, kids, pets in action.

- 1/2000–1/4000 → Birds in flight, fast wildlife.

- Bulb/20s+ → Long exposures, night sky.

Aperture Reminders

- f/1.8–f/2.8 → Shallow background blur, low light.

- f/4–f/5.6 → General portraits, balanced depth.

- f/8–f/11 → Landscapes, sharp detail front to back.

- f/16+ → Sunbursts, maximum depth, but watch for diffraction.

Shortcut: Need a quick safe setting? ISO Auto, f/5.6, shutter 1/250 sec covers most casual shooting.

Autofocus Setup Cheat Sheet

AF Modes:

- **One Shot AF:** Still subjects (portraits, products, landscapes).

- **Servo AF:** Moving subjects (kids, sports, wildlife).

Detection Modes:

- **Face + Eye AF:** For people portraits.

- **Animal AF:** Dogs, cats, birds, wildlife.

- **Tracking AF:** For unpredictable motion.

AF Area Selection:

- **Single Point AF:** Precision — products, macro, still subjects.

- **Zone AF:** Moving subjects, casual action.

- **Wide Area / Full AF:** Sports, birds, fast unpredictable motion.

Shortcut: For moving subjects → Servo AF + Eye/Animal Detection + Zone AF. For still subjects → One Shot + Single Point AF.

Video Setup Cheat Sheet

Resolutions & Frame Rates:

- 4K Fine (Oversampled) → Maximum detail, cinematic look.

- 4K Standard → Balanced quality, longer recording times.

- 1080p → Smaller files, casual content.

- 120 fps (1080p) → Slow motion.

Frame Rate Guide:

- 24 fps → Film look.

- 30 fps → Standard smoothness (YouTube, interviews).

- 60 fps → Sports, action, extra smooth motion.

- 120 fps → Dramatic slow motion (no audio).

Profiles:

- **Standard:** Ready-to-use, vibrant colors.

- **C-Log3:** Flat, cinematic, needs color grading.

Audio Tips:

- Always use an external mic (shotgun or lav).

- Monitor sound with headphones.

Shortcut: For YouTube → 4K Standard, 30 fps, Standard profile, shotgun mic.

Lens & Accessory Cheat Sheet

Lenses by Genre:

- **Portraits:** RF 50mm f/1.8, RF 85mm f/2.

- **Travel:** RF-S 18–150mm, RF 24–105mm f/4.

- **Landscapes:** RF 16mm f/2.8, RF 15–35mm f/2.8L.

- **Wildlife:** RF 100–400mm, RF 100–500mm.

Must-Have Accessories:

- Tripod → Landscapes, video, night sky.

- ND Filters → Long exposures, cinematic video.

- Extra Batteries (LP-E6NH) → Essential for long shoots.

- Fast UHS-II Cards (V60/V90) → Smooth 4K and burst shooting.

- External Mic → Clean, professional audio.

Shortcut: Start with RF-S 18–150mm (travel) + RF 50mm f/1.8 (portraits) + tripod + spare battery.

Closing Thoughts

Cheat sheets don't replace full learning — they condense it. Use these as quick reminders in the field, especially when you don't want to fumble with menus. Over time, these choices will become second nature, but until then, keep this chapter as your "ready reckoner."

The EOS R7 is at its best when you don't overthink settings but let intuition and preparation guide you. These one-page guides are here to help you stay focused on the shot, not the buttons.

Quick Reference Cheat Sheets

ISO/Exposure Guide

ISO   Shutter Speed   Au

☀ 100   1 1600   3200

Fast   AF

Use as exposure triangle to balance light, motion, anddeth

Autofocus Cheat Sheet

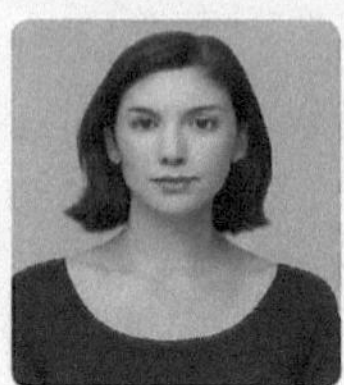

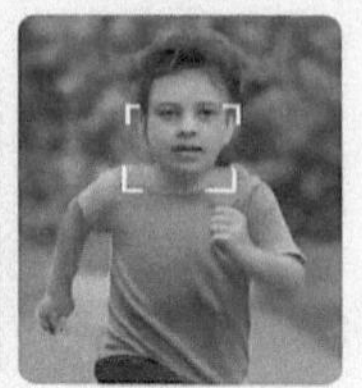

One Shot   Servo AF
+ Ey AF   + Zone AF

Choose AF modes based on whether subjects are still or

Video Cheat Sheet

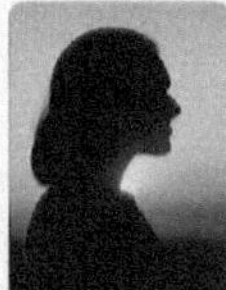
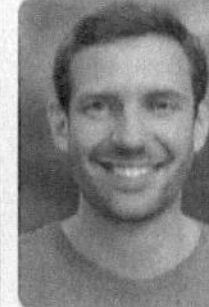
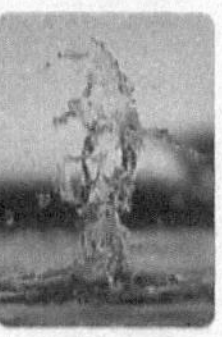

CINEMATIC   SMOOTH   SLOW
LOOK   YOUTUBE   MOTION
24 fps   30 fps   120 fps

Frame rate sets the mood: cinematic, smooth, or dramatic slow motion

Lens & Accessory Quick Picks

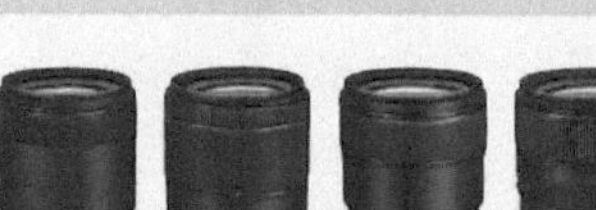

Portrait   Travel   Landscafe

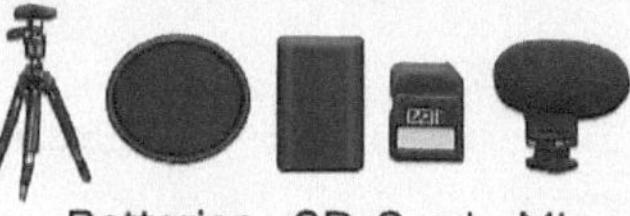

Batteries   SD Card   Mic

EOS R7

Glossary of Key Terms

Aperture – The adjustable opening inside a lens that controls how much light enters. Smaller f-numbers (like f/2.8) = wide opening, more light, blurred background. Larger f-numbers (like f/11) = narrow opening, less light, more of the scene in focus.

Auto ISO – A setting that automatically adjusts ISO based on lighting so you don't have to.

Bracketing – Taking several shots of the same scene at different exposures, so you can choose the best one or combine them later.

Buffer – Temporary storage inside the camera that holds images before writing them to your memory card. If you shoot too many images quickly, the buffer can fill up and slow the camera.

C-Log (Canon Log 3) – A flat video profile that records maximum detail in shadows and highlights, designed for editing and color grading.

Depth of Field – How much of your image is in focus from front to back. Controlled mainly by aperture.

Dynamic Range – The camera's ability to capture details in both bright highlights and dark shadows.

Exposure Compensation (EC) – A control that lets you quickly make an image brighter (+) or darker (–) without changing manual settings.

FPS (Frames per Second) – How many frames (photos or video images) your camera captures per second. Higher fps means smoother motion or faster bursts.

ISO – A measure of how sensitive the camera's sensor is to light. Low ISO = clean image in bright light. High ISO = brighter in low light but more noise.

ND Filter (Neutral Density) – A dark filter placed in front of a lens to reduce light. Used for long exposures (waterfalls, skies) or video in bright daylight.

Oversampling – Recording video at higher resolution (like 7K) and downsizing it to 4K for sharper, cleaner footage.

Servo AF – Autofocus mode that continuously adjusts to track moving subjects.

Shutter Speed – How long the camera's shutter stays open. Fast = freezes motion. Slow = shows blur or allows long exposures.

Time-Lapse – A sequence of photos taken at intervals and combined into a fast-motion video.

White Balance (WB) – A setting that makes whites look truly white under different kinds of light (daylight, tungsten, fluorescent, etc.).

Acknowledgments

Creating this guide has been a journey made possible by more than just technical know-how—it's been powered by community, curiosity, and countless moments behind the lens.

First, to the everyday photographers—beginners, seniors, travelers, vloggers, and creators—who inspired this book: thank you. Your questions, frustrations, and breakthroughs shaped every chapter and reminded me why clarity matters.

To the online communities, forum contributors, and real-world Canon EOS R7 users who openly shared their challenges and insights: your stories breathed realism into this work.

A special thanks to my editorial team, design collaborators, and research assistants for helping bring structure, precision, and visual support to every page.

Finally, to the readers picking up this book—whether you're just unboxing your Canon R7 or finally ready to leave auto mode behind—thank you for trusting this guide as part of your journey. May it help you create images that not only look beautiful, but feel meaningful.

Keep shooting. Keep learning. The world is waiting through your lens.

About The Author

Randy Osborn is a trusted name in the world of camera education, known for transforming complex gear manuals into simple, step-by-step guides that anyone can understand. With over a decade of experience working hands-on with leading camera systems—from Sony and Canon to Nikon, Leica, and more—Randy has helped thousands of photographers, content creators, and everyday users get the most out of their cameras without the overwhelm.

Driven by a passion for accessible learning, Randy creates user-friendly books that strip away the jargon and focus on real-world usage. Whether you're shooting your first vlog, learning manual mode for the first time, or simply trying to take better family photos, Randy's guides are designed to make every setting click.

Each book combines clear instruction, practical tips, and

relatable language, making it easy for beginners and seasoned hobbyists alike to master their gear and capture life with confidence.

When he's not writing, Randy enjoys field testing new camera releases, hosting beginner-friendly workshops, and exploring hidden photography gems across the globe.

Join the journey to sharper skills and smarter shooting— one page at a time.